GOD &
FOOTBALL

GOD & FOOTBALL

FAITH AND FANATICISM IN THE SEC

CHAD GIBBS

ZONDERVAN®

ZONDERVAN.com/
AUTHORTRACKER
follow your favorite authors

We want to hear from you. Please send your comments about this book to us in care of zreview@zondervan.com. Thank you.

ZONDERVAN

God and Football
Copyright © 2010 by Chad Gibbs

This title is also available as a Zondervan ebook. Visit www.zondervan.com/ebooks.

This title is also available in a Zondervan audio edition. Visit www.zondervan.fm.

Requests for information should be addressed to:

Zondervan, *Grand Rapids, Michigan* 49530

Library of Congress Cataloging-in-Publication Data

Gibbs, Chad.
    God and football : faith and fanaticism in the SEC / Chad Gibbs.
        p. cm.
    ISBN 978-0-310-32922-0 (softcover)
    1. Southeastern Conference. 2. Football—Southern States. 3. Football—Religious aspects—Christianity. 4. Football—Social aspects—United States I. Title.
    GV958.5.S59G54 2010
    796.332'630975—dc22   2010019707

Cover design: *Jeff Gifford*
Interior design: *Matthew Van Zomeren*

Printed in the United States of America

---

11 12 13 14 15 /DCI/ 23 22 21 20 19 18 17 16 15 14 13 12 11 10 9 8 7 6 5

For Tricia

CONTENTS

PRESEASON

THE SEASON

POSTSEASON

PRESEASON

GOD AND FOOTBALL

WELCOME TO THE AMERICAN SOUTH, where God and football scrimmage daily for the people's hearts and minds.

Perhaps you think this an overstatement. Perhaps you should exchange this book for one you can color in. (I'm sorry; that's an awfully mean thing to say to someone who just bought your book.) Think of it this way: suppose an alien were to visit Tuscaloosa, Knoxville, or Baton Rouge—and if you don't believe in aliens, you can substitute a Canadian. Suppose this visitor—we'll call him Corso—were to spend a week observing the ordinary citizens of those towns. What do you think Corso the alien would conclude about the religious beliefs of those average, everyday people?

Well, on Sunday morning he'd probably see them make their groggy, wrinkled-shirted way to a steepled building where some sort of ceremony had begun ten minutes before they arrived. Inside, he'd watch as they mouthed the words to songs, then struggled to stay awake while a man spoke for less than twenty-five minutes. Then, for the rest of the week, this place would be the furthest thing from their minds, unless by chance something tragic happened.

Corso might be justified in concluding that church, for most, was a court-ordered punishment.

On Saturday, Corso would see something completely different. The people would wake up early, carefully choose an outfit based on the good fortune it had brought them in the past, then drive, sometimes for hours, to a hallowed campus where some sort of ceremony is scheduled for much, much later that day. All afternoon they would eat, drink, and fellowship with friends, family, and strangers. Then, when the time came, they would all enter a colossal shrine and join tens of thousands of similarly dressed and likeminded people. Inside, they would chant and sing until they lost their voices, and afterward they would celebrate like they're at a wedding reception on Fat Tuesday.

After he sees this, I think it's safe to say Corso will think he's found the one true religion—and he'll probably convert on the spot.

Football is big down here in the South. Real big. From peewee to junior high, high school to college, and even the NFL, southerners love their football. And the fans of the Southeastern Conference (SEC) are arguably the most ridiculously passionate fans in America. Consider: each spring nearly half a million fans attend spring practice games at the twelve SEC schools. Did you catch that? *Practice* games. This year alone, more than six million people will witness an SEC game in person, tens of millions more will watch on CBS or ESPN, and at least a dozen will read this book.

Football is a cash cow for the SEC's institutions of higher learning. This year, the combined athletic budgets of the twelve schools exceed 800 million dollars. That's more money than the GDPs of twenty-four of the world's poorest countries. Granted, I don't know what GDP stands for, but this figure sounds impressive nonetheless.

● ● ●

But before you start feeling too bad for God, I want you to know he's doing okay down here as well. In a nation that has historically considered itself Christian, the southern states are by far the most Christian-y. A 2004 Gallup Poll that tracked religious affiliations state by state showed that in eight of the nine SEC states, over 86 percent of people considered themselves Christians.[1] I began to scour the Internet for a poll that wasn't six years old but lost focus after I discovered peopleofwalmart.com.

Of course, not all people who tell Gallup they are Christians are what other Christians would consider Christian — they might not even follow John Piper on Twitter, know the words to "Shout to the Lord," or invite friends to see Kirk Cameron movies at their church. Granted, Scripture is silent on the part social networks play in salvation, but clearly at least some of the 86 percent of self-reported Christians are nothing of the sort. Perhaps they just picked up the phone one night in 2004, and when someone asked if they were "Christian" or "Other," they chose the former. Christianity, believe it or not, is the southerner's default setting.

● ● ●

So we've established that God and football are both pretty big down here, but which is bigger? Well, I've got a theory.

When you attend a church here, you will almost certainly hear people talking about football. Worshipers will gather before the service and discuss in reverent tones what went right and wrong the day before. The pastor will usually reference Saturday's happenings by either praising a team's win or mourning its loss, while oftentimes taking a playful dig at the misfortunes of a rival school.

---

1. Despite the best efforts of Tim Tebow, Florida checked in at a measly 81.6 percent.

Churches sometimes encourage this blending of faith and fanaticism with "wear your team's colors" day or by having viewing parties for big games—with halftime testimonies, naturally.

Conversely, God doesn't get a lot of play in SEC stadiums, unless a player injures his neck or your team is lining up for a last-second field goal. And sometimes God is called upon to do some damning—usually of referees or offensive coordinators—but that's it. The SEC doesn't really have to add God or anything else to their product to fill the seats. There is no "wear your denomination's colors to the game" day.

Churches have to schedule around football. Apart from tailgates and viewing parties, a church event planned on Saturday in the fall is guaranteed to be a colossal failure. So far as I can tell, the SEC does not have to consult the churches when it makes its schedule. It makes sense to me that if one thing has to schedule around another, then that thing isn't as important to the people participating.

Apart from Christmas and Easter, only tragedy gives churches those SEC-like attendance numbers they so greatly desire. The first weekend following September 11, all twelve SEC stadiums sat empty, while the churches were filled to capacity. Of course, depending on national calamities isn't really the best strategy to increase church attendance, but what can churches do? The people have chosen today what they will worship, and it looks like God is a two-and-a-half touchdown underdog to the Tigers, Bulldogs, and Gators.

The people have chosen. You'd think I wasn't part of the problem ...

OTHER GODS BEFORE ME

> I grew up in Alabama—perhaps the worst place on Earth to acquire a healthy perspective on the importance of spectator sports.
>
> *Warren St. John*

I WAS IMMERSED IN THE WATERS of Southeastern Conference football twelve months before I was submerged into those of believers' baptism. This is not a unique testimony, at least not in the South, where the age of accountability is often preceded by the age when your parents are sure you can sit through an entire game without crying. Two weeks before my ninth birthday, I was thrown into the backseat of my Uncle Jimmy's station wagon and taken to Legion Field, where I watched Satan's minions from LSU defeat my beloved Crimson Tide.

The majority of the blame for that 14–10 loss was placed on my perceived-to-be-unlucky shoulders, which explains why I was not invited back to a game for the next three seasons. I say that's why, but I suppose it could have been my insistence on taking a sack full of G.I. Joes into the stadium. Lucky for me, Bill Curry would eventually lose enough games that my family had to admit that not *all* of Alabama's misfortunes were a direct result of my childish indifference.

So at the age of twelve, my family started throwing me back in my uncle's station wagon and driving me to either Birmingham or Tuscaloosa, where I'd watch the Tide destroy some hapless foe. And it was always the hapless foe. I had apparently been deemed too much of a risk to take to another conference game. This was fine with me, because a win was a win—who cared if it came at the expense of the Biloxi School of Hotel Management and Massage Therapy? Besides, I was with Uncle Jimmy and Grandpa James, the two men not named MC Hammer I admired most when I was twelve.

For the next few seasons, my family's strategy of taking me to games without putting the Tide's win-loss record at risk worked like a charm. I witnessed the thoughtless slaughter of under-manned teams from Cincinnati and Tennessee–Chattanooga. But even this almost backfired when I nearly ruined Bama's 1992 national championship season with my attendance at the Louisiana Tech game.

This was a game that shouldn't have been close. The Crimson Tide's defense was stacked with future first-round draft picks, and their offense, while not very exciting, hadn't to this point had any trouble scoring points. But late in the game, heavily favored Alabama was clinging to a harrowing 6–0 lead. Fortunately for me, and the team of course, David Palmer returned a fourth-quarter punt for a touchdown and cemented the uninspiring win.

Driving home, I listened while Jimmy and Grandpa discussed in spectacular hyperbole just how bad this year's team was.

"If we can't move the ball any better, we won't win another game."

"I'm not sure we'll ever score again."

"We should probably disband the team."

Always the optimist, I tried to interject a little hope into the conversation: "David Palmer is awesome! Right?"

Jimmy and Grandpa just looked at me, then continued with their assessment of what was, apparently, the most abysmal team to ever don the crimson and white.

"I know one thing," Jimmy started up again, "there's no way we beat Auburn playing like that."

This caused me to throw up in my mouth. Auburn was our archest of archrivals, and each year we had to play them in a game known simply as the Iron Bowl. I'd spent most of my school career absorbing verbal blows from Auburn friends who were wallowing in the ecstasy of a four-game winning streak over Alabama. The Tide had turned in 1990, and for the past two seasons I'd been learning to spew insults right back. It had never occurred to me that losing to Auburn again was even possible. I thought the travesty of the late eighties was akin to God destroying the earth with a flood, and Gene Stallings was our rainbow. (If you think that analogy is stretching things, just keep reading.)

Of course Alabama didn't lose to Auburn that year, or to anyone else. The Tide beat Florida in the inaugural SEC Championship Game and then destroyed Miami in the Sugar Bowl to capture the national championship. Jimmy brought me back all sorts of loot from the game and even gave me a VHS copy of the broadcast. I spent hours watching and rewatching the big plays, eventually wearing out those parts of the tape so it sounded like Keith Jackson was calling the game in his own made-up language: "Tuckdrown Maladrama!"

That season, and that game in particular, cemented a couple things for me. First, I was now an Alabama football fanatic. Sure I cared before, but now it consumed me. I began memorizing the depth chart, a gateway drug to harder stuff like preseason magazines, which I soon began studying like Scripture. Then, worst of all, I started paying attention to recruiting, which satisfied my craving to care about football every day of the year.

The other thing 1992 did was convince me my uncle Jimmy was the coolest man to ever live. Now I know what you are thinking, and before I go any further, I want to set things straight: I was not some fatherless child whose male relatives took turns escorting to sporting events. I have an amazing father, but his autumns were devoted to that other southern pastime: white-tailed deer hunting.

I could have gone either way because I sort of like the idea of sitting in a tree and taking out God's creatures with a high-powered rifle. What I didn't like, and what in the end sealed my fate as a football guy, was cutting those creatures open, hacking out their innards, and separating the gross edible parts from the purely gross parts. My time as a deer hunter was short-lived and rather uneventful, unless you happened to be the one deer I shot in the face, in which case it was very eventful.

So I was a football guy, not a deer guy, and that brings us back to Jimmy. The man went to all the games. He witnessed the goal-line stand in 1979. He saw Van Tiffin's kick in 1985. He was in New Orleans for the 34–13 trouncing of Miami, and he was the first adult I knew to have a room in his house entirely devoted to cool stuff. The walls were covered with signed pictures, programs, posters, and jerseys. He had cardboard stand-ups of players, signed bats and balls, and a filing cabinet full of celebrity autographs he'd collected through the years. Anytime we'd visit, I'd run straight to this room and try not to drool on the memorabilia.

What I didn't know at the time, but would soon learn, was that Jimmy also struggled with addictions. This was scary stuff for a fifteen-year-old. I couldn't talk to Jimmy about it; I wasn't even sure I was supposed to know. But that summer at church camp I came up with a plan: I'd pray for him.

This plan was actually a joint venture with my best friend, Ryan, whose brother Jeffery, at one time or another, had been addicted to just about every substance known to man. Spending the night at Ryan's house was always exciting because you never knew when Jeffery would stumble in the door, stoned out of his mind. Depending on the drug du jour, he would either sit and tell us funny stories or chase us around the house with a shovel.

Ryan and I bugged each other to pray every day for God to change our loved ones. We both believed God would answer our prayers, and soon all would be right in our worlds.

On the gridiron that fall, Alabama fell back to earth, while Auburn went undefeated. Most years this would have been enough for me to take drugs myself, but I sort of figured God was making Alabama crappy because he was going to fix my uncle. (It's understandable when a teenager thinks like this; what's scary is I still do it in my thirties.[1]

By the following spring, Ryan and I had been praying for nearly a year. Since Ryan was an Auburn fan and his team went undefeated, it made sense that my prayers would be answered first, but God soon tore the roof off this theory.

March 27, 1994, is a day people in northeast Alabama will always remember. On that day, twenty-six tornados ripped through parts of Alabama, Georgia, South Carolina, and North Carolina. Twenty miles from my hometown, the meanest of the lot slammed into the Goshen United Methodist Church, collapsing the roof and killing twenty worshipers. That morning our pastor stopped the choir during their opening hymn and told us of the imminent weather. He decided to have an invitation, then quickly dismiss us to go seek safety. The organist played "Just as I Am"

---

1. And not just football. If we don't tithe, I fully expect our car's alternator will go out within five days. I must be one of those Christians who believed in Karma in a past life.

a little faster than we were used to, but before she could finish, Ryan's brother Jeffery stood up and walked down the aisle. It was one of the most beautiful things I have ever seen. We all anxiously rejoiced with Jeffery and his family, and when we thought the moment had been adequately celebrated, we ran for our lives.

My answer came a couple of months later, early Sunday morning, July 31, 1994.

At the time I was high on God, following another week at church camp. And I was filled with hope after seeing Ryan's prayers answered before my eyes. That Saturday night, I prayed to God, giving him my list of wants and wishes, writing them down in my prayer journal, and then I fell asleep.

My grandparents lived next door to us, and the police went to their house first. When they told my grandmother her son Jimmy had been killed in a car accident, her screams woke up everyone on our block. I almost thought it was a dream, until our phone rang. Since no one calls after midnight to give you good news, I jumped out of bed in a panic. Mom was already awake, and she beat me to the phone. When she answered, I could hear my grandmother's screams over the phone and across the yard at the same time. Before Mom ran next door, she told me what had happened. I didn't cry; I just stood there feeling numb. It's strange, but immediately after the moment that would dramatically change my life, I crawled back into bed and fell asleep.

When I woke up the next morning, I walked next door, and for the first time in my life I saw grief in the eyes of people I loved. My grandmother was an empty shell, sitting at the kitchen table, staring through the walls. Grandpa James sat in his recliner, holding a towel over his eyes to hide his tears. It rattled my soul and awoke in me an anger I hadn't known existed. Seeing them like that was too much for me, so I went back home and got dressed for church. Mom told me I didn't have to go if I wasn't up to it, but I had something I needed to do.

At church I was smothered with hugs and told by everyone that they would be praying for me. I smiled, thanked them, then took my seat, waiting like a prizefighter for the bell to ring. Nothing in the sermon reached my heart, and when the pastor opened the invitation, it was on. I walked the same aisle Jeffery had walked three months before, knelt at the same altar, then prayed the kind of prayer that could get you struck by lightning. When I finished scolding God, I asked him one question: Why? I had played by his rules; I prayed just as hard as Ryan. So why did he kill my uncle? When God didn't explain to me why Jimmy had died, I decided to have nothing to do with God until he did.

● ● ●

Five weeks after Jimmy died, Alabama took the field to open the 1994 season. The first game was against UT–Chattanooga, the game Jimmy and Grandpa would have taken me to, but Jimmy was gone, and though I didn't know it, Grandpa would never attend another Alabama game. So I watched the games on TV or listened on the radio and was pleased with the Tide's 4–0 start, even if I was feeling a little apathetic toward the world in general. Then came the Georgia game and a 21–10 halftime deficit. After watching those first thirty minutes, I would have bet anything the Tide was beat, but Jay Barker[2] went nuts in the second half, throwing for 396 yards and two long touchdown passes. And when Michael Proctor's field goal attempt with a minute to play split the uprights, the Tide had completed an incredible comeback win.

While driving home, I listened to the postgame radio show, which is generally a forum for the hardest to please people in the world to voice their displeasure with everything.

"Hey, guys, longtime caller, first-time listener. Look, I don't want to second-guess Coach, but some of our pregame stretches

---

2. Mr. Sara Evans to you country music fans.

look a little feminine. You think we could find a more manly way to work our hamstrings? I'll hang up and listen."

I usually can't handle those shows, but that night I was too happy to get mad at the morons. So I turned up the volume and reveled in the postgame idiocy. Then it happened. While coming back from a commercial break, the first notes of "Yea, Alabama," the Crimson Tide's fight song, came through my speakers. I had to pull over. And sitting there on the side of the road, I cried for ten minutes. I missed Jimmy so much. He would have loved that game.

Something weird happened to me that night. It was like all aspects of my life—faith, family, football—began to blend together into some quasi religion that only I knew about. I think most people agreed something special was happening for the Tide, but people always say things like that when a team goes on an unexpected run or has a few comeback wins. I was taking things a step further, however, and was actually convinced God was willing Alabama to win, or at least Jimmy was in God's ear encouraging it. This belief was cemented after another comeback win at Mississippi State, then a twenty-one-point first quarter against Auburn. God was going to give Bama the national championship to make up for the death of my uncle.

The Tide met Florida for the third straight year in the SEC Championship Game. It was an incredible game full of back-and-forth scoring, and with just under five minutes to play, the Gators took the lead, 24–23. I knew Jay Barker would lead the Crimson Tide down the field for yet another miraculous victory; I knew God was helping the Tide.

Except he wasn't. And Barker didn't. Florida picked off a Barker pass, and the game was over. I felt like I'd been kicked in the stomach. How could this happen? Why was God doing this to me?

I thought we'd had a deal. In my mind, God would give Bama

the national title, I'd forgive him for killing my uncle, and we'd call it even. Now I thought God was just playing with my emotions on top of killing my relatives, so I called things off with the Almighty.

For the next four years, I only attended church at my mother's tearful requests. I didn't read the Bible, and I only prayed when I had a sick relative—and even then I couldn't help but feel God was going to once again use my prayers as a sort of insider knowledge to bring me pain.

Football remained a big part of my life during those angry-at-God years, although Alabama was never quite the team they were in the early nineties. Then in 1997, Gene Stallings retired and Mike Dubose was named head coach. Dubose promptly led the Tide to their worst season in forty years. Everything I loved brought me misery.

Nevertheless, in February of 1998 I opened my acceptance letter to the University of Alabama. After all those years, I was actually going to be an Alabama student. Some friends and I visited campus to find an apartment, picked one close to the Krispy Kreme, then made plans to go back with our parents in two weeks to sign the lease. Then something strange happened.

A few of my friends from high school were students at Auburn, and for months I'd been saying I would come visit them. The week before our lease signing, I drove south on Highway 431 and spent a couple days down on the Plains. I loved every second of it.

I've never been fully able to explain what happened, and I don't expect I'll be able to here, but Auburn, I guess, just felt like home. I felt safe there. I felt that no matter what was going on in the world, as long as I was in Auburn, I would be okay. I remember driving home and my mind was already made up. Of course I was going to college at Auburn. Somehow I'd always known it.

"I think you'd better unknow it before I smack you."

My mother didn't quite share the peace I had about my going to Auburn. My dad, however, was okay with it, and in the end my folks agreed it wouldn't *quite* be the end of the world if I went to college there.

I frantically applied to Auburn, got accepted, got an apartment, got a major I had no business being in,[3] then got two Fs and a new major. But academic failures notwithstanding, I was happy in Auburn, even though I was still a huge Alabama fan. I kept cheering for the Tide mostly out of loyalty to Grandpa James. He'd already lost his son, and I thought losing me, even figuratively, would be too much for him. Of course Auburn going 3–8 my first year, their worst record since 1952, didn't provide much incentive to switch colors.

Perhaps just as shocking as my going to Auburn was that I started going to church again in Auburn, though not for spiritual reasons, unless you consider things done to impress a girl spiritual. At first I was just going through the church motions, but one particular Sunday morning something odd swept over me, and before I knew it I was down at the altar again, begging God to forgive me for being such an idiot.

I was born again, again, and my second honeymoon with God lasted all of about four weeks — until the aforementioned girl decided we should just be friends. This put me at a crossroads, because a part of me couldn't help but think God had tricked me into talking to him again. Okay, *all* of me thought that. But I also realized I had no one else to turn to for comfort. I wasn't living at home anymore, where my mom could make me soup and tell me there were plenty of fish in the sea. Besides, after I decided to go to Auburn, she wouldn't do that anyway. I was far away and all alone.

---

3. Engineering. In fact I had five majors in my first five quarters at Auburn: engineering, architecture, business, history, then finally philosophy.

So instead of turning away from God, I turned to him, and he was there for me when I needed him most. I don't know what to call this: it was sort of like when Butch and Sundance jump off that cliff, even though Sundance knows he can't swim. I wasn't sure what would happen, but I knew I'd be with God, and soon we'd be running from the law in Bolivia. Or something.

What I mean to say is that our relationship deepened, and since then I've tried consciously to live my life for God. I know that sounds like religious gobbledygook, but I don't know how else to say it. I mean, it's not like I've been perfect since 1998, but since then I've tried hard to live a life that would make God proud. I guess I'm saying that the effort has been there, even if the results haven't always been.

I realize we're getting into chicken-or-the-egg territory here, but with my spiritual awakening came a decline in interest toward Alabama football. Of course I was in Auburn now, going to Auburn games with my friends, so I wasn't really watching the Tide much, but I still tried to keep up with the goings on in Tuscaloosa. I was excited in 1999 when Bama captured the SEC title, and I was disappointed in 2000 when Bama opened the season ranked third in the nation, only to win three games the entire season. But somehow I didn't care as much. I had other things going on. My joy didn't come from a game being played by guys my age I'd never met.

This era of keeping football on the periphery combined with a steadfast, though sometimes misguided, devotion[4] to God was perhaps the best three-year period of my spiritual life. The idol of football had been removed, and I was free to be the person God was calling me to be.

---

4. About this time I became convinced God wanted me to go to seminary and become a preacher. One year as a part-time youth minister helped convince me that wasn't the case.

Then it happened.

I remember the exact moment I knew I was becoming an Auburn fan. It was the summer of 2001. I was working at an FCA golf camp, and I remember thinking before I left that I wanted everyone I met to know I was an Auburn student. I bought a decal for my car, a T-shirt for my back, and a visor for my head. When I got back, I began reading up on Auburn's team in those dreaded preseason magazines. I told myself it was just one peek—totally harmless.

When the first game rolled around, I was in the student section wearing my new Auburn T-shirt. I remember the neck on it itched, and my friend Patrick, who doubted the sincerity of my conversion, said the shirt could tell I was a hypocrite.[5] I had my doubts too, but by the fourth game of the season I was actually cheering for South Carolina to beat my beloved Crimson Tide. I couldn't help it. It wasn't something I consciously decided to do. If I now wanted good things to happen to Auburn, I had to now want bad things to happen to Alabama. South Carolina won 37–36, and I was strangely satisfied. Two weeks later Auburn played host to the #1-ranked Florida Gators. The game was close throughout, and when Damon Duval made a forty-four-yard field goal to win the game for Auburn, I was done for. Auburn football had now taken the place of God, who had just recently taken the place of Alabama football in my life.

Ridiculous, I know. Like going on a diet, only to replace French fries with doughnuts. But at least this time I didn't abandon God altogether. I still went to church; I still prayed; and I still loved God. But that place in my heart where I kept what was most

---

5. It should be noted that my girlfriend at the time, the one who now shares my last name, is a huge Auburn fan. She likes to take full credit for my conversion, and she probably deserves at least some acknowledgment, but I think most of the change can be attributed to the transformative work of the Holy Spirit.

important to me—well, God and Auburn football were sharing a bunk bed.

Mom found out at Thanksgiving when I wore an Auburn T-shirt home during the holiday break. She was not thrilled. Grandpa wasn't thrilled either, but at least he didn't die of grief like I'd feared. He did, however, inform me that when he did meet his demise, his other, more *loyal* grandchildren would be inheriting his Alabama memorabilia.

Over the next few years I lived and died with my Tigers. I became more fanatical than ever, in part to make sure my Auburn friends knew I was truly an Auburn fan, and in part because relapses are always worse.

In 2001 I suffered the humiliating loss to Alabama on Black Saturday;[6] I was encouraged by the 2002 campaign; I was distraught by the debacle of 2003; and then, in another strange concoction of God and football, I became convinced God was an Auburn fan in 2004. But at least that time I wasn't alone.

Auburn got off to a hot start that year, and after one of the wins, perhaps the blowout of Tennessee, the football review showed our players singing an old spiritual called "Hard Fighting Soldier." A song about "bringing souls to Jesus." Of course, that is why we were undefeated. God was on our side. We beat Georgia and Alabama, we won the SEC for the first time in fifteen years, and then we won the national championship! No, wait, that's not exactly what happened.

Oklahoma and USC were also undefeated that season. Seems God loved them, too. Problem was God did not understand how the current BCS system works,[7] and he must have thought all three teams could somehow play for the national title. So I guess

---

6. This meant I was, most likely, the only fan in the world to cheer for the losing team in both the 2000 and 2001 Iron Bowls.
7. This is understandable, even for an all-knowing deity.

as far as God was concerned, we were all number one, but as far as computer nerds went, Auburn was number three, and we had to watch USC and Oklahoma play for our national championship.

Now twice God had guided my teams through undefeated seasons, only to break my heart in the end, once because I thought he was picking on me and now because he didn't factor in strength of schedule. Questions began to arise as to why I do this to myself—meaning of life–type stuff—but I mostly ignored them. This was in part due to our three-game winning streak over Alabama, which extended to four in 2005, then five, then a record sixth win over the Tide in 2007.

Then came the 2008 season. Auburn's Book of Job. How bad was that season? Well, an early 3–2 win over Mississippi State was a highlight. No, that wasn't a typo.

When that season finally ended with a 36–0 loss to Alabama, everything was over. My winning streak over the Tide, my immunity from rival-fan smack talk, my reason for living—everything. Auburn fired Tommy Tuberville, its coach for ten seasons, then hired Gene Chizik, who despite rumors of being a nice guy and good father had a 5–19 record as a head coach. Recruiting suffered, and all hope was abandoned. I spat in the face of optimism; I urinated in the cornflakes of hope.

Losing makes me introspective, which means Vanderbilt fans must be the most self-aware people on earth. (Yes, Vanderbilt beat Auburn in 2008 too.) But when my team crashed in such incredible fashion, I had to step back and ask, Why is this so important to me? Why do I spend all my money to go watch something that only makes me angry? And why do I waste so much of the precious time I've been given eating, sleeping, and drinking a game played by college kids I've never met? Couldn't and shouldn't that time be spent on eternal things?

And as a Christian I have to ask, Why do I worship something that I know will let me down when I could be worshiping a God that I know never will?

Usually such questions linger only until your team signs a five-star QB prospect and you leap off the back of the wagon. But this time was different for me. At first I thought I was starting to like football less, but I had my doubts about that being the case. I mean I *did* like it less, but you always like it less when your team is losing. I think what was happening, maybe, was that I *wanted* to like football less. Or, to put it another way, I wanted to like God so much that football would naturally fall into its proper place.

This was a scary desire, because we've all known people who are so godly that things like football, *Star Wars*, and video games mean nothing to them. In public we praise these people for being so spiritual; privately we pity them because we think their lives must suck. I don't want my life to suck.

What I want is to be the kind of person who can enjoy college football without worshiping it, even though I'm not really sure what that means. I know I want to go to games, and I want to scream like a madman, and I want to celebrate victories like I somehow contributed. But I don't want to wish death or worse on rival fans, and I don't want to feel physically ill when my team disappoints—and I never, ever want a game to keep me from being the person God has called me to be.

When I say it out loud, I'm not even sure it's possible, at least not for those of us who truly love this game. But surely, somewhere out there a Christian has figured out how to keep his or her fanaticism from hindering faith.

I just have to find that person and ask how it's done.

THE QUEST

"I'M GOING TO SPEND the next three months traveling to football games."

Can you imagine saying those words to your wife? Even as a joke? Even when she's asleep? Well, I did, and her response was amazing: "Okay, but I'm going with you on the fun trips."

Of course, others had their doubts. "You just want to see a bunch of great football games," was the common response. This was a logical conclusion, albeit a false one. Sure I'm a football fan, but I'm an *Auburn* fan, and a pretty rabid one at that, so the thought of driving to Lexington to watch Kentucky play Mississippi State when I could be in Auburn for the Ole Miss game was, if anything, a downer.

What ultimately got me packed and out the door was people — people like me who love their team and love their God but are doing a better job than I at separating and prioritizing the two. So in the summer I began emailing churches and campus organizations around the SEC in hopes of finding people I could learn from. People who are passionate about their team but don't mistakenly pray to their head coach at night.

The response was faster than Herschel Walker. I talked to people from all over the South. Many shared my predicament, but others seemed to have found perspective through the years. I was encouraged to know there was hope for the crazed fan, and to know at least I wasn't the craziest of the crazies.

So in August I printed out all twelve SEC schedules and spread them across our dining room table. With markers and poster board, I got to work on what I thought would be the easiest part of the book. I was wrong. The problem was that I wanted to see Auburn as often as possible, which proved to be a disservice to the other schools. For instance, if I saw Auburn play in Baton Rouge, I'd get stuck watching Florida play Charleston Southern. If you are not familiar with Charleston Southern, just picture your high school team with smaller players. So with a heavy heart I marked through some Auburn games I would not be attending and eventually settled on my twelve-week run through the conference. Now it was time to start taking trips.

I decided each week I'd leave on Friday and drive my 1999 Honda Accord to a different SEC school. Some nights I'd stay with folks I'd spoken to, other nights I'd stay with friends, and if all else failed, I'd get a hotel room. At each stop I'd try to soak up the sights and sounds of a typical football weekend, all the while spending time with rabid Christian fans like myself. I'd attend the game, no matter how hard a ticket was to find, and on Sunday I'd worship with a local church, each week visiting a different denomination.

What follows is what happened as best as I can remember. You'll notice I tried not to bog things down with too much school history. If you're an Alabama fan, you know why your mascot is an elephant; and if you're not an Alabama fan, you probably couldn't care less. (If however, after reading this, you can't sleep because you don't know why LSU's mascot is named Mike,[1] then I suggest you look into something called the Internet.)

---

1. He was named for fictional TV architect and father of six, Mike Brady.

So get ready for the no-holds-barred action of the greatest football conference in the history of time, where every game provides enough heroic material for a dozen epic poems. In this league there are no easy wins, there is only guerrilla warfare on freshly mown grass. Welcome, my friends, to the SEC, where every game is more important than everything else in the world, combined. We start with ... uh ... we start with Western Carolina at Vanderbilt?

THE SEASON

WEEK I

VANDERBILT UNIVERSITY

SEPTEMBER 5, 2009

You rarely win, but sometimes you do.
Harper Lee, To Kill a Mockingbird

VANDERBILT ISN'T THE MOST LIKELY PLACE to open a book about SEC football—it's like starting the Bible with Philemon. But I had to start somewhere, and after weeks of scheduling and rescheduling, the best possible route through the conference had me beginning in Nashville at the Vanderbilt–Western Carolina game. At least Vanderbilt fans, who should still be basking in the glow of their first bowl win since the Eisenhower administration, would be pumped for their season opener. Wouldn't they?

My friends didn't think so. More than one person told me it wouldn't matter which game I went to because Vanderbilt didn't have fanatical fans. Vanderbilt had, at best, a small group of people who, through a series of unfortunate events, would accidentally show up at the stadium. My first email reply seemed to confirm this.

Chad, I regret that we water down the rabid qualities of our members pretty quickly, both regarding their faith and their football.

Sincerely, Rev. Ken Locke,
Downtown Presbyterian Church

It turns out Rev. Locke was joking, at least about the watering down part, but he really didn't have any fans at his church who could help, and after a week without hearing from anyone in Nashville, I began to wonder if perhaps my friends were right. Until I got an email from Father John Sims Baker.

Father Baker is the chaplain for Vandy+Catholic, a student ministry on Vanderbilt's campus. He also holds the distinction of being the first priest I ever spoke to.[1] We talked about football and the tribulations of cheering for the Commodores, then I asked if his passion for Vandy ever hindered his relationship with Christ. "No," he said. "Being a lifelong Vanderbilt fan helps you to accept the cross." Blessed are the poor in tackling, I guess. Then Father Baker told me about a Dominican Sister who was also a big fan of the Black and Gold. I wanted to ask if she'd taken a vow of disappointment but thought that would be rude, so I just thanked him for the lead and went to investigate.

Being a Southern Baptist whose knowledge of nuns comes exclusively from Whoopi Goldberg films, I assumed the sister was actually from the Dominican Republic. A friend of mine named Wikipedia told me I was an idiot, and that the Dominicans are a Catholic religious order founded by Saint Dominic in 1216. It turns out this sister was actually from Tennessee, which made much more sense.

I looked up the convent and called Sister Commodore one afternoon, but as the phone rang, I began to panic. I realized I'd never

---

1. This is really just a guess. I'm sure I could have spoken to an undercover priest at some point in my past, but how would I know?

spoken to a nun before. In fact I'd only seen a handful in real life, and those seemed like very serious women. Certainly not the type that would want to discuss football with me. How often do men call a convent anyway? What if the Mother Superior answered and thought I wanted to ask one of the nuns on a date? I realize now, in the calm of my office, that this line of thinking was ridiculous. But that day I hung up as soon as someone answered the phone.

A few weeks later I regained my nerve and called the convent once more. Another sister answered the phone, Sister Gamecock perhaps, and I could swear I heard a football game playing in the background. I asked for Sister Commodore, and when she came on the line I introduced myself. She was very kind and passed up the chance to point out my idiocy when I said I didn't realize nuns were allowed to watch football. "Of course we can watch football," she said. "We are watching Alabama and Arkansas right now. I'm afraid Dont'a Hightower just severely injured his knee." I wanted to talk to Sister Commodore longer, mostly so I could ask her about the religious implications of completing a Hail Mary, but the television in the background grew louder, which I took as a sign the other sisters were ready for her to get off the phone so they could enjoy the game. So I said good-bye, then sat back and imagined this group of nuns sitting around a television yelling at a football game. That's when I realized this football season was going to be even more eye-opening than I'd imagined.

●　●　●

On Friday, September 4, I left work at 3:30 and drove north on I–65 toward Nashville. I'd only been there twice before — once to watch Auburn play in the Music City Bowl and once to see the Rockettes kick their glorious legs in celebration of Jesus' birth.

I arrived on campus a little before 7:00, slightly apprehensive because I'd agreed to spend my first night in a house full of fraternity guys. I called Andy Enkeboll, a Vanderbilt senior who'd arranged my night at Animal House, but he had some bad news.

"Yeah, that place fell through. I'm talking to some of the brothers to see where else I can put you. I'll call you back in a bit."

These brothers Andy referenced were members of Beta Upsilon Chi (BYX), a Christian social fraternity that has chapters at twenty-five universities in the United States. The idea of staying in a house full of frat guys should have set off some alarm in my head, but, sadly, I had been operating for the past nine years under the false impression that I had not aged since college. This delusion wouldn't last thirty minutes into my three-month journey.

While waiting on Andy, I called another Vanderbilt senior, Jonathan Payne, who is an active member of Reformed University Fellowship (RUF), and the president of something called Vandy Fanatics, the school's one and only spirit organization. It's Jonathan's job to encourage his fellow students to care about Commodore athletics, and it's their job to ignore him.

When I called Jonathan, he was at the Kickoff Cookout, a student-only welcome-back-to-school event just down the road from where I'd parked. "Come on down, I can sneak you in," Jonathan said. So I went.

Knowing I'd be hanging out with students, I'd dressed the part. Long-sleeved shirt, untucked, with the sleeves rolled up, and a pair of faded jeans hanging over my gray New Balance sneakers, which are standard issue at SEC schools.

Jonathan met me at the entrance to the cookout, and I was shocked to see he was seven years old. Okay, that's a lie, but he was much younger looking than I thought a college senior could be. He snuck me in past what I assumed were off-duty girl scouts checking student IDs, and I was just floored by the fresh-facedness of it all. When did I get so old?

Standing there like a Rolling Stones fan who mistakenly bought tickets to Miley Cyrus, I nodded as Jonathan explained the intricacies of Vandy Fanatics marketing efforts.

"It's a lot like *Clockwork Orange* really. We tape their eyelids open, administer some IV medicine, then make them watch films of libraries exploding."

"That's great," I said absentmindedly. "Where did my life go?"

Jonathan gave me a strange look and said he had to go since it was time for his welcome address to the freshmen. "But you're welcome to come to the pep rally after the cookout," he added. I said thanks, but declined. I needed to find someone who looked older than me, and quick.

Walking on a strange campus is always a little disorienting, especially at night, but fortunately for me I spotted a large group of gray-haired people walking toward a bright light a couple blocks away. I followed them if not for any other reason than to feel better about my age, and it turns out they were going to watch a women's soccer match.

During the six years I lived in Auburn, I saw exactly zero women's soccer matches, but it had to beat sitting in my car, so I paid five bucks and went inside. Vanderbilt was playing Belmont University, another Nashville school best known as the alma mater of Beyoncé.[2] The Lady Commodores were already up 2–0 by the time I bought a hot dog and found a seat, and just as I was about to start a soccer riot, Andy called back with some rather distressing news.

"Sorry man, the guys didn't have any room for you. Looks like you'll be staying in my dorm."

In the grand scheme of things, I suppose a dorm room floor was better than a park bench, and both were better than a frat house couch, so I lied and said this would be great.

---

2. Yeah, I made that up, but I didn't have time to Google Belmont.

Andy said he was about to go run—from what, I could only imagine—and that he'd meet me at the soccer field afterward. So I watched the girls from Vandy play keep-away from the girls from Belmont until I saw a tall, sweaty guy I assumed to be Andy.

Meeting someone you've only known electronically is always awkward. We stood behind the Belmont goal making small talk about soccer, something I am only capable of making small talk about. I assume Andy was trying to assure himself that if he let me stay, I wouldn't throttle him in his sleep. This is only natural, as I was wondering the same thing about him. Eventually we felt safe enough to head back to his dorm. That, and we'd run out of things to say about soccer.

Andy lived in Carmichael Towers, a series of fourteen-story high-rise dormitories on the edge of campus. At the entrance a security guard checked my ID and most likely assumed I was Andy's father coming to inspect his room for drugs.

We took the elevators up a few floors, and upon entering Andy's dorm, I was knocked back by the thumping bass of a Kanye West album. Four guys sat on two couches playing some sort of war game on an Xbox 360. Andy attempted to scream an introduction over the chorus of "Gold Digger," but no one looked up.

"Well," Andy said, "make yourself at home. I'm going to take a shower and get ready."

I sat down in a chair in the corner of the room and watched the four guys shoot each other until the game ended and they noticed I was there. "So you're the book guy?" one of them asked.

"Yeah," I said. "Are you guys in BYX with Andy?"

"No," one of them said, almost laughing. "We know Andy from Original Cast."

"Original Cast?"

"Yeah, it's Vanderbilt's musical theater group."

"Oh." I followed up with little expectation, "Are you guys big sports fans?"

"I'm a huge South Carolina fan," said a guy named Oliver.

"Kentucky hoops," said another kid named Andrew.

"What about Vanderbilt?" I asked, slightly confused.

The guys explained that most Vanderbilt students have a second team, usually the team they grew up cheering for, that they still keep up with. Fan adultery, if you will. They all cared about the Commodores but had seen enough misfortune to know a backup school wasn't a bad idea.

"What about when Vanderbilt is playing your other team?" I asked.

"We cheer for Vanderbilt."

I was happy to hear this and told them since I'd never actually been to a game at Vanderbilt, I was glad I'd be there for a win.

"Shut up!" they screamed in unison. Seems they'd all been there long enough to not take anything for granted.

About that time dozens of guys came pouring into the room. Some of them were singing a song from the musical *Wicked*,[3] and before long I found myself in a strange conversation with a little guy from New Orleans.

"Why are you here?" he asked, a little too bluntly.

"I'm writing a book."

He looked skeptical.

"It's about Christian faith and football fanaticism in the South."

He thought for a second then said, "Dude, I *love* all that [stuff]!"[4] I wondered if that would be a better front- or back-cover endorsement.

We talked about Hurricane Katrina for a bit, and then I confessed that until just recently I'd been under the impression I could seamlessly blend in with college kids.

"No way, man, you're like, really old looking."

---

3. Shut up. My wife makes me listen to the soundtrack on trips.
4. Zondervan made this edit. You can guess what he really said.

"Thanks."

"Think about it," he said. "I mean, how old do I look to you?"

"I don't know, eleven maybe."

"See, you're old."

This little guy wasn't making me feel better about things, so I went to find Andy. He was in his room, wearing clothes that made him look homeless. I almost commented, but that would have been an old-person thing to do, so I bit my tongue.

"What's going on?" I asked.

"'Bout to head out," Andy said. "There's this party thing going on."

I glanced at the clock. It was close to 11:00 p.m. On most nights I would have been asleep an hour ago. In the living room, the rest of the guys were turning off the Xbox and getting ready to go out as well. At first I was a little hurt that no one even considered asking if I'd like to join, but then Andy said, "You're welcome just to sleep in my room tonight. I probably won't be back till pretty late."

I decided being asleep in a bed before midnight was much better than spending the next four hours playing the part of creepy old guy at a college party, so I wished them a good evening and went to bed. Sleep did not come easy, however, as the Carmichael Towers are located directly across the street from Fraternity Row. I tossed and turned as parties raged on eighty feet below. Even after I fell asleep, my dreams were troubled because I was in a strange building, and the roof, the roof, the roof was on fire. Then, like the old person I am, I woke up at 6:00 a.m. and couldn't fall back asleep.

Andy was asleep on the couch, and I tried to tell him I was going to find some breakfast and that he could have his bed back. He made a noise that didn't really sound human and rolled over. Walking back to campus after breakfast, I passed Nashville's to-scale replica of the Parthenon, which looks as odd as you'd imagine the Parthenon would look in Nashville. A homeless man approached and asked for some change. I gave him a couple of bucks, and he asked what I did for a living.

At a wedding a few months earlier, when small talk inevitably turned to vocations, I finally got up the nerve to tell a group of strangers that I was a writer. Now I was even more comfortable making this assertion, particularly with this unusually inquisitive vagabond I'd never see again.

"I'm a writer," I said, feeling both literary and philanthropic.

"Me too," he replied, and pulled a beat-up paperback from his front pocket. I looked at the book, then had a terrifying flash of my future, a future in which I'm homeless, begging for change in front of misplaced ancient ruins, with a copy of the book you are now reading in my front pocket. I quickly walked back toward campus.

At 9:30 I met Joe Thomas, director of Vanderbilt's Campus Crusade, for a cup of coffee. We'd spoken on the phone a few weeks earlier, and Joe was, in a word, intense. Well, not intense about everything, but very intense about Vanderbilt football.

Joe's kid wouldn't sit still at Starbucks, so we decided to go for a walk. Strolling through campus, Joe pointed out buildings and told me their names, which I immediately forgot, then we came to an open area by the library, and Joe said, "This is where ESPN's *College GameDay* set up when they were on campus last season."

He was referring to Vanderbilt's home game against Auburn, which at the time was being called the biggest home game in Vanderbilt history. "I woke up that morning at 4:00 a.m.," Joe said. "I couldn't go back to sleep, so I just drove to campus and nervously walked around." Of course Vanderbilt won that game—something Joe took pleasure in reminding me of—and then went on to win their first bowl game in more than forty years.

We made our way over to Vanderbilt Stadium, which holds 39,790 fans—by far the smallest in the SEC. Joe led us through a gate, waved at a security guard, and all of a sudden we were standing on the field. This blew my mind. It was game day at an SEC stadium, and we just walked onto the field. Had this been anywhere else, attack dogs would have been eating the three of us, but here we just took some pictures and strolled around like we owned the place.

Walking back, I asked Joe if his passion for football ever caused him to say or do something he would later regret.

"Definitely. Many times. Most of all it affects the way I look at people. I judge them. If I see people wearing UT orange, I automatically want to say things to demean them."

Then Joe went on to tell me about his near arrest in Knoxville after a particularly tough loss to the Vols. "I refused to yield for the referees and their police escort after the game. This Knoxville policeman kept telling me to move, and I nearly yelled something I would have regretted. But thankfully I came to my senses."

Listening to Joe's stories, I began to feel a tinge of panic. I'd sort of been banking on Vanderbilt fans being able to offer me a better perspective on sports; instead I'd gotten nuns gathered around a TV watching football and campus ministers standing down police escorts. What chance does a guy like me have if even clergy struggle with the balance?

But maybe I *was* changed, I kept telling myself. Auburn's losing season had taught me some things about myself, and surely I wouldn't slip back into my old ways, even if the Tigers were to look good in their season opener, which was taking place 330 miles away at the same time as Vanderbilt's game.

By then we were back at Joe's car, and he told me to make sure I found him during the game. This is when I realized that perhaps I had not properly planned my trip. It was only noon, and I didn't have anywhere to be for four hours. I decided to walk downtown and find a sports bar where I could eat lunch and perhaps watch a few games.

Walking down Twenty-first Avenue, I noticed a line wrapping around a restaurant called the Pancake Pantry. It was lunchtime, over 90 degrees, and I had serious doubts that anyone would be standing in line for pancakes. Perhaps Kenny Chesney was inside autographing pancakes.

After lunch and a two-hour nap in the student union, I made my way across campus to meet up with Jonathan Payne and the rest of his Fanatics. Even though Vandy students support football about as well as Sudan supports its bobsled team, the one person you cannot blame is Jonathan Payne. No one works harder to make his fellow students care about the Commodores.

When I arrived at the tailgate, two guys with matches and a can of lighter fluid were trying, rather carelessly, to light a massive grill. Once the charcoal caught, the can of fluid was doused on the flame, making an impressive fireball that drew some applause from neighboring tailgates. Minutes later the fire was out, and the scene would repeat itself for the next hour or so.[5] Carrie Fry, another hardworking Vandy Fanatic, was setting up a table of free stuff for students. Then for the next two hours she watched the table like a hawk, making sure students, and only students, took the swag. I thought about grabbing a T-shirt, but after seeing Carrie swoop in to keep an old woman from a pencil, I decided against it.

Around 6:00 Jonathan said we should go back to his dorm and get my ticket. This scared me. Not only was kickoff in thirty minutes, but his dorm was way across campus. Did he plan on missing kickoff? We took off walking, past the stadium, where people were starting to file in, toward the dorms. Everyone we passed seemed to know Jonathan.

---

5. Years from now when this book is taught in freshman English classes, teachers will undoubtedly have students write essays comparing the fading fire to the Commodore fan base.

"Hey, Jonathan," they'd say.

"Hey, whoever," he'd reply. "Are you going to the game?"

"No, sorry," they'd answer, with what appeared to be genuine remorse. You'd think all this rejection would start to wear on him, but Jonathan remained upbeat. He would probably make an excellent telemarketer.

We picked up my ticket, Jonathan changed into a gold shirt and gold shorts,[6] and we walked back toward the stadium. It was seven minutes till kickoff when we passed the SAE house, and a party was raging in the front yard.

"What in the world," I said. "Are they not going to the game?"

"We're a late-arriving crowd," Jonathan informed me. "They'll be there, probably mid–second quarter, then they'll leave middle of the third."

I immediately thought of that Bible verse, "We played the flute for you, and you didn't dance; we played football for you, and you didn't cheer." Or something like that.

Just as the Commodores kicked off, we took our seats in what was, thanks to Jonathan Payne, a pretty rowdy Vanderbilt student section. The students began doing cheers I'd never seen or heard, most of which incorporated a hand motion that looked similar to Mr. Spock's Vulcan salute. This would be a common occurrence throughout my journey. I would try to learn the cheers, but I was always a few words and at least one hand motion behind. Also I'm pretty sure the fight song contained the line, "Down the field with blood to yield," which sounds more like a Red Cross slogan than anything else.

Five minutes into the game, Western Carolina and Vanderbilt had combined for three fumbles. It was not pretty. I began to wonder if perhaps I had jinxed the Commodores with my bold prediction of a victory, but Larry Smith saved me when he hit Justin

---

6. Would a C-3PO joke be too nerdy for a sports book?

Green on a long pass, which the latter bobbled two or three times before hauling it in for the score. By halftime Vandy was up 21–0, and the game looked well in hand.

Sometime during the third quarter, I made my way over to see Joe Thomas, who, despite the commanding Commodore lead, was very upset about everything. Joe only stopped critiquing the players to critique his fellow Vandy fans who had decided this would be a good time to do the wave. "Pay attention!" Joe shouted to no one in particular.

During a timeout we discussed Vandy's freshman tailbacks, Zac Stacy and Warren Norman, who were both approaching 100 yards on the ground. "We've had some solid recruiting classes the past two seasons," Joe said. "Of course, we've still been dead last in the SEC."

Vanderbilt won the game 45–0, to the delight of those of us who stayed till the end. Walking back to the dorms, Jonathan told me I could check the Auburn score on his computer. "Oh, we won 37–13," I said. I'd only spent half the night watching it on my phone.

Back at Jonathan's dorm, there was no thumping bass, no parties to get ready for, just a few guys sitting around watching television. My delusions about fitting in with college kids slowly began to creep back into my graying head.

Later I asked my new friends their thoughts on the rest of the season. Most SEC fans I know go into each season convinced ten wins are guaranteed, but not these Vandy fans.

"I think we can win six games again," Jonathan said. "Get in another bowl game and maybe win seven."

"We'll win four games," Jonathan's friend Steve deadpanned.

I guess hope doesn't spring eternal everywhere.

We said our good nights and went to bed. I was exhausted, and even the parties raging down below couldn't keep me awake—in fact tonight they seemed to be singing me to sleep. *A little bit softer now, a little bit softer now, a little bit softer now.*

Driving to church the next morning, I passed the Pancake Pantry, which once again had a line wrapped around the building. The guys had informed me that people did in fact stand in line for hours just for pancakes, and that I would too if I had ever had them. I wanted them this morning but didn't have time, so I ate next door at a place called Fido's, which was delicious. In fact, if you are in Nashville and don't have an hour to wait, just eat breakfast at Fido's and tell people you had Pancake Pantry.

That morning I went to church at West End Community Church. This is where Joe Thomas worships. It is a Presbyterian church (PCA).[7] Joe was scheduled to work in the nursery that morning, which worried me a bit after seeing him in action the night before. He met me before the service and introduced me to a few folks, one a former linebacker for the Commodores.

"You go to the game yesterday?" Joe asked him.

"Was it a home game?" the linebacker replied.

I thought Joe was going to tackle him.

The inside of the church didn't look like what I'd typically call a church because it was what I'd typically call a basketball gym. In my seat I actually had one foot on the three-point line, and I could hear my high school coach screaming, "Gibbs, that's the worst shot in basketball!"

The music at West End was impressive. But when you consider one out of every two people in Nashville is trying to break into the music industry, this wasn't unexpected.

Pastor Carter Crenshaw's sermon was part thirty-two of a series called "One Magnificent Man." Yes, part thirty-two. It was

---

7. Anytime I meet someone who goes to a Presbyterian church they always say "PCA" really quickly after they tell me the name of their church. Being a Baptist, I don't know what this means and don't really care, but they are so consistent I felt the need to include it here.

an excellent sermon, with two pages of very extensive notes, driving home all my stereotypes of Presbyterian pastors.

Afterward I went to the nursery to say good-bye to Joe. He was holding a sleeping baby and said good-bye to me in a whisper that sounded odd coming out of his mouth. Seemed he could switch off crazed-fan mode—a good thing for everyone, particularly that baby.

Driving home, I tried to reflect on the weekend. Sure I met a few fans with the famed Vanderbilt apathy toward football. Pastor Crenshaw even asked if I knew who the Commodores played *after* I told him I went to the game, leading me to believe he knew fans who could go to a game and never even notice an opposing team. But there were just as many folks like Joe Thomas and Jonathan Payne, who were every bit as fanatical as fans from other schools. And who knows, if Vanderbilt were to win a few SEC titles, I imagine the indifference would fade as the bandwagon filled up.

I guess I was hoping these Vandy fans with the high-dollar education and low-dollar athletic budget could teach me how to remain blissfully detached from the highs and lows of my football team, but the ones I talked to were no better than me. Seems I can only achieve that blissful detachment when Auburn is so bad I don't want to be attached to them. In fact, looking at mile marker after mile marker pass outside the window, I could think of nothing but our 37–13 win. Later that night, while I was watching our game on TiVo, I began to let myself wonder if perhaps this team was special. Maybe God was going to let Auburn win them all because I was finally taking a critical look at the role football plays in my life.

One day into the season and my healthy perspective had already disappeared. Looked like I had a confession next time I spoke to Sister Commodore.

WEEK 2

AUBURN UNIVERSITY

SEPTEMBER 19, 2009

And I wonder, still I wonder, who'll stop the rain?
Creedence Clearwater Revival and
the Auburn Student Section

WHEN I HAD MY ~~DAMASCUS~~ WIRE ROAD conversion from Crimson-
ism to Auburnantity, it was more than a superficial changing of
T-shirts. My conversion was Pauline in every sense, except the
sense of going blind. Like Paul, who spent three years studying in
Arabia, I too took some time to become acquainted with my new
religion. For me this involved learning the fight song, memorizing
statistics, and watching tapes of old Auburn games until I eventually got goose bumps during highlights that once brought me to
tears. How that last point is even possible I don't know, but who
among us can fathom such mysteries?

As I've already told you, my family didn't exactly welcome
news of my conversion with open arms. In fact, I'm fairly certain
I could have converted to Scientology with less scrutiny. During a

family Christmas gathering in 2001, my mother insisted on telling our relatives that I'd come out of the closet. Gasps filled the room. She laughed and said she meant I was now an Auburn fan, and the gasps were louder still.

I think everyone back home would have eventually forgiven my apostasy had I kept my orange and blue light under a bushel, but instead I became the worst kind of Auburn fan: an evangelical one. I took every chance to corner my younger, impressionable cousins and tell them all about "The Loveliest Village on the Plain." Soon they were visiting me at school, and before long I had my first convert. It wasn't just any convert, either; it was Melissa, oldest daughter of my Uncle Jimmy. For me this was the equivalent of talking the pope's daughter out of going to Notre Dame.[1] Melissa started cheering for Auburn on her visits and eventually got up the nerve to wear her Auburn gear back home, thus cementing her place in Grandpa James' will, right next to me.

I, James Parrish of Glencoe, Alabama, being of sound mind and broken heart, do hereby bequeath to my traitorous grandchildren, Melissa Parrish and Chad Gibbs, any expired food found in my refrigerator at the time of my death.

After her high school graduation, Melissa enrolled at Auburn, pleasing me greatly and sending shockwaves through my family. But nothing could have prepared me for what happened next.

Remember my father, the woodsman who, so far as I knew, worshiped at the altar of Bear Bryant? Well, he came out of the closet too. (I really need a better metaphor.) What I'm trying to say is that my dad became an Auburn fan.

"Oh, your dad's always been an Auburn fan," my mom informed me. "He just cheered for Alabama because everyone else in the family did. You were all he needed to go back to that side."

---

1. And before my Catholic friends start sending nasty emails, I know, the pope's daughter would have to go to college in Italy.

You were all he needed to go back to that side. I was Luke Sky-walker. I saved my father from the dark side.

That is where things stand now. On one side you've got me, my father, a few cousins, and my grandmother, about whom my family used to whisper like she was a Communist. On the other side you've got, well, everyone else. So in the span of a year I divided what was once a happy, crimson family.

● ● ●

The years I spent at Auburn were the most formative years in my relationship with Christ, and consequently the school means a great deal to me. I think many of us feel that way about our time at college, though for some Christ took a backseat to a budding relationship with fermented malt.

I met some of my dearest friends at Auburn—seven of my eight groomsmen went there—and it was in Auburn that God gave me the love of my life. A redheaded firecracker who, according to her best friends, "wasn't looking for anything serious." We've been together now for nine years, and to make sure she stays happy, I'm rarely serious about anything.

So you see, when I think of Auburn, I don't just picture a building or a football team. When I think of Auburn, I think of friends I will have for life. I think about Tricia, and how I used to sit up at night wondering if she was sitting up thinking of me.[2] And most important, I think about a young me discovering the joys of an intimate relationship with my maker. It's really no mystery why I love Auburn, and it's no wonder that, when I tell people about my alma mater, I want them to love it the way I do.

Never was this more evident than when I flew Jordan Green in from Phoenix to see the Auburn–West Virginia game.

---

2. She wasn't.

● ● ●

In 2006 I became the last person in America to read Donald Miller's bestselling book *Blue Like Jazz*. Inside the back cover was a link to an online magazine Don founded called the *Burnside Writers Collective*. I visited the site and soon became a contributor, which is how I met the site's editor, Jordan Green. Jordan was not only the editor, he was also Don's former roommate, and after I submitted one of my better pieces, the two of them called and convinced me to write a book. So I wrote a book and for the next thirty months lived through an absurd series of events that culminated in a book deal from Zondervan. But then I pitched this book, and Zondervan decided they'd rather publish it. So my first book, I suppose, was put in storage like the Ark of the Covenant at the end of the first Indiana Jones flick.

Jordan was instrumental in that first book deal, but he wasn't working for me in any official capacity. So when I got paid, he did not, and this seemed like a great injustice. So to repay Jordan for all his help and hard work, Tricia and I decided to fly him out to Alabama and take him to an Auburn game. We checked our schedules, and more important, checked his wife, Mindy's, due date for the impending birth of their first child, then determined the West Virginia game had to be the one. So on Friday, September 18, I drove to the Birmingham-Shuttlesworth International Airport and met my friend Jordan for the first time.

Originally from Portland, Oregon, Jordan is a Pac-10 guy, especially the Oregon Ducks. If you are not familiar with the Pac-10, it is a football league/reality show that only allows seven players on defense and requires quarterbacks to carry purses. If this sounds intriguing, you can watch their games Saturday nights on Bravo. The SEC, on the other hand, is a manly league, full of men's men. Just look at our head coaches—in ages past they would have been gladiators or gunslingers. We're talking about big, daunting men like Urban Meyer and Nick Saban ... Okay, so our coaches aren't what they used to be, but at least we still play defense.

I fully intended to convert Jordan into a born-again SEC fan by Sunday, and I started by taking him to Dreamland BBQ on Friday night. We sat down and ordered drinks, then Tricia and I watched eagerly as Jordan took his first sip of authentic southern sweet tea. With one swallow he was both refreshed and prediabetic.

While waiting on our pulled-pork sandwiches, Tricia asked Jordan about his wife and unborn daughter and all the other things girls think to ask. I asked him about the Oregon Ducks and was skeptical when he told me how loud Autzen Stadium was. No one in the SEC likes to hear how loud other team's stadiums are, especially when they only seat 54,000.

"Is it louder than a concert?"

"Whose concert?"

"I don't know, Kenny G."

"Yeah, probably."

"Is it louder than a jet engine?"

"How far away is the jet engine?"

"Within arm's reach."

"Yeah, probably."

This went on for some time, until we were rudely interrupted by a bolt of lightning hitting the restaurant. The power blinked, came back on, then went out for good. We sat in the dark listening to the distant wail of weather sirens and wincing every time the sky exploded in electrical bedlam.

"Does it do this often?" Jordan asked.

"Every now and then," I said. "But I'd rather it rain tonight, because that means tomorrow should be beautiful."

So of course we woke up Saturday morning to a driving rain. This was no good. Everything needed to be perfect if I was to convert Jordan, and spending a rainy day under a tent was far from ideal. It'd be like inviting a Jewish friend to your church, only to find your pastor was out of town and Mel Gibson was the guest speaker. I quickly pulled up the radar online and determined, by way of self-taught meteorological expertise, that the rain was already north of Auburn, and campus should be dry for the rest of the day. The drive down from Birmingham, however, was going to be a little soggy.

Soggy turned out to be an understatement. There were times during the two-hour drive when I couldn't say for certain if we were still on Highway 280, or if I'd missed a turn and we were driving around the bottom of Lake Martin. Tricia and Jordan were both voicing doubts about my forecast (to be honest I was starting to wonder myself), but then we crossed into Lee County. Lo and behold, the sun peeked through the clouds, and the Lord did grin.

"I told you!" I yelled, though Jordan didn't seem impressed, and Tricia reminded me it was still very early in the day and just because it wasn't raining now didn't mean it wouldn't rain later. Humbug.

On most trips to Auburn these days, Tricia and I take back roads to avoid game traffic. But you wouldn't use a side door to show a guest around heaven, so that day we drove straight down College Street to give Jordan the full experience. I watched his face to see if the small-town quaintness of College Street, or the redbrick majesty of Samford Hall, would convert him on the spot. It did not.

"Have you got the music?" I asked Tricia.

"Yep, right here!"

Tricia inserted a CD marked "Fight Songs" and thus introduced Jordan to perhaps our strangest tradition. Not an Auburn tradition, a Tricia and Chad tradition. Every time we travel to watch the Tigers play, we listen to, in order, the following songs:

"War Eagle" (The Auburn fight song)

"Glory, Glory to Ole Auburn"
"Tiger Rag"
"Eye of the Tiger" (Yes, the eighties song)
"War Eagle" (Yes, the same as #1)
"H to the Izzo" (Yes, by Jay-Z)
The Jay-Z song is on there because I made the fight song CD back in the days of illegal Napster, when all your CDs were a hodgepodge. Auburn won the first time we played it, thus cementing our belief that the songs always had to be played and in this order. Sure, Auburn lost some games after we played the disc, but think how much worse the losses would have been if we hadn't done our part.

After finding a parking spot of questionable legality, we unloaded our tailgating chairs, and I introduced Jordan to the gang. Our tailgating group has been together in the same spot since the season opener in 2003, a 23–0 loss to eventual national champion USC. That first tailgate consisted of ten people sitting on shipping crates and eating pretzels in the baking sun. For entertainment we watched fire ants crawl up our legs. Today about thirty of us sit in foldout recliners under half a dozen orange and blue tents. We eat from a banquet table laden with BBQ, fried chicken, and dozens of family dip recipes. For entertainment we have a generator that powers our forty-two-inch plasma television, which, thanks to our satellite dish, broadcasts hundreds of channels in glorious high definition. We've come a long way, baby.

At the tailgate Jordan met my friend David Shaul. David and I met on an Internet site that ranks seventeen-year-old boys. Wow, that sounded sketchy! Let me try again: We met on auburnsports. com, an Auburn recruiting message board that ranks the top high school football stars. Somehow David and I became good friends, and he's been a fixture at our tailgate for years. He is also Jewish, which you wouldn't know by the amount of pork he consumes at our tailgate. I had David explain to Jordan why this was okay while he was filling his plate with pork tenderloins wrapped in bacon.

"First of all," David began, "pork wrapped in bacon cancels each other out."

"Fair enough," Jordan said, not really being an expert on Hebrew dietary laws.

"And besides," David said, placing a tenderloin in his mouth, "my rabbi told me everything is kosher at a tailgate."

While Jordan was becoming acquainted with the rest of the crew, Tricia and I discussed how the day had progressed. We decided Jordan hadn't traveled quite far enough down the road to enlightenment, so we took him for a walk around campus. First stop was Samford Hall, Auburn's stately main building, and the place where I proposed to Tricia. We offered to reenact the magic moment for Jordan, but he took a pass. Next up was Toomer's Corner, the spot where Auburn University and the city of Auburn intersect. On the campus side of the corner stand two live oak trees that, in one of the strangest traditions in college football, get covered in toilet paper after every Auburn victory.

We walked across the street and went inside Toomer's Drugs, which, despite the name, doesn't actually sell drugs. But they do sell their world-famous lemonade, and I bought Jordan a small glass. He eyed it a bit skeptically.

"Just try it," I said. "But slowly."

It's the same every time you see a person take his first sip of Toomer's lemonade. First his eyes widen. Most people are not used to so much pleasure and pain at one time. Then his face relaxes a bit, and his eyes roll back in his head as an expression of pure bliss washes over his face. Wait, I'm thinking about a Swedish massage. But people like the lemonade, too.

On our way back to the tailgate, we met up with Rachel Winter, associate pastor and campus minister at First Presbyterian

Church of Auburn (PCUSA).[3] Rachel is among a growing number of female pastors in Alabama, which brings the total of female pastors I know up to two.

We found her and her family tailgating just outside First Presbyterian. I thought tailgating at a church was a little odd, but Rachel explained the benefits. You have great parking, a shady spot under the steeple, and easy access to clean church bathrooms. Point taken.

Rachel told us how she was born into the Auburn family. "My grandfather played here, his face is on one of the murals outside the stadium. He used to lay down the law to us grandkids, saying if we were going to be Auburn fans, then we would have to act like Auburn men and women."

"What do you mean Auburn men and women?" Jordan asked.

"It's a family thing," I said, and Rachel nodded. "But not always something that is passed down generation to generation. I'm in the Auburn family, but I came by it a much different way than Rachel. I think really it means you are part of something bigger than yourself. When you go out in the world, you are representing Auburn, and when you need help, you know Auburn people will have your back."

Jordan nodded, though I'm not quite sure he got it, and walking back to our tailgate, I started to understand why.

"What you were describing as the Auburn family," Jordan said, "is really what the church is supposed to look like."

When I thought about it, he was right. In fact I think Auburn sometimes does a better job of being the church than the church does. Walk around campus on a game day wearing orange and blue, and you will certainly feel loved and that you are part of something big. At tailgates we welcome and feed strangers, something

---

3. Again with the Presbyterians. But I will say PCUSA sounds more patriotic. I'll assume they are the conservative ones.

that almost sounds biblical. As a matter of fact, at least once a day I see someone post a prayer request on an Auburn sports message board, where dozens of Tiger fans promise to lift up prayers on their behalf. Perhaps it's no wonder I wanted to evangelize Jordan so bad; in many ways Auburn had become my church.

● ● ●

Back at the tailgate I piled a gravity-defying stack of fudge brownies onto my plate and sat down next to Jordan, who was engaged in a conversation with an Auburn student friend of ours named Kyle Bradberry.

Kyle told us he was planning to leave on a yearlong mission trip next summer. The trip, from what I could tell, was sort of like *The Amazing Race*, but you replace finding clues with leading people to Christ.

"Wait, you are going to miss an entire season of Auburn football?" I asked.

"Yeah, that's going to be the hardest part."

"Missing your family won't be the hardest part?" Jordan asked.

"No, I can talk to them on Skype whenever I want. But Auburn games are at a set time, and there is no way to know if I'll be able to watch them."

I was impressed with Kyle, because if I'm being honest, it's not something I'm sure I could do. Missing Auburn games to watch other football games already felt like a huge sacrifice; leaving the country for a year felt borderline fanatical. Our friend Brooke Culpepper spent the fall of 2004 in South Africa working at an orphanage, and not only did she miss the entire football season, she missed Auburn's 13–0 SEC championship football season. What if I left the country and we won the national title; wouldn't I regret it for the rest of my life? Or maybe it would be the best fall of my life; Brooke still talks about 2004 like it was the best of hers.

Kyle went on to explain that after a painful loss in 2008 he had a sort of epiphany. "I was walking back to my apartment and felt sick to my stomach. Then it was like God said to me, 'This is what happens when trivial things become too important.' It was kind of liberating. I mean, if I don't let football get too big, it can't hurt me."

I don't like it when a twenty-two-year-old kid points out just how shallow my life is, but I like Kyle, so I decided not to banish him and his healthy perspective from our tailgate. The thing is, he wasn't telling me anything I hadn't already learned at least a dozen times, but my fear has always been if I don't let football get too big, will I still be able to enjoy it? Sure, I get depressed when my team disappoints, but what about the high I get from a win? Where would I go to replace that feeling?

● ● ●

Night games make for long tailgates, and as the afternoon slowly ticked by, we passed the time with cornhole[4] until it was time for Tiger Walk. Over the next few months, I would learn that every school has a walk, be it the Vol Walk, Dog Walk, or Hog Walk. I know we like to take credit for this trend, and since I'm not about to waste time actually researching, I'll add to the precedent and say it started at Auburn.

Tricia, Jordan, and I made our way down to the corner of Roosevelt and Donahue to join the masses waiting to greet our undefeated football team. There was an excitement that had been missing since the previous year's fiasco and everyone knew a win tonight could mean big things for the Tigers. But just as the band arrived to lead the spirit barrage, the skies blackened, and soon thousands of formerly excited people were soaked and angry.

---

4. This might need some explanation. Cornhole is a game played by tossing bean-bags into holes on raised platforms. To learn more, you can use Google, but be careful!

Apart from ferry rides under Niagara Falls, there is nothing you can do that is enhanced by doing it in a poncho—and Tiger Walk is no exception. It was hard to hear the band or the cheers, it was difficult to see the players as they rushed by to the shelter of the stadium, and when it was over, it was hard to tell anyone apart, because everyone had apparently bought the same bright orange ponchos for $3.95 at a gas station in Alexander City. Tiger Walk at times is one of the most exciting traditions in college sports, but that day not so much, and when it was over, Jordan let out a big yawn.

After another hour of tailgating, the time had come to disassemble our tent city and journey to the stadium. We jostled for position at one of the entrances, passed through security with minimal frisking, and then hustled down the concourse while children begged us to buy programs. Fighting through the commotion, we finally made it around to Section 42, and we watched Jordan walk through the tunnel into the 87,000-seat stadium.

I've walked through that tunnel hundreds of times, but still it overwhelms me. The scoreboard lit up like the Vegas strip, the opposing bands whipping their respective cheering sections into a frenzy, and the people—so many people—everywhere you turn. In fact, on game days Jordan-Hare Stadium becomes the fifth largest city in Alabama. I glanced over to see if Jordan's jaw had dropped appropriately, and it had, so we took our seats and wondered aloud why there seemed to be so much nervous energy in the air. Turns out it had something to do with the giant electrical storm forming in the western sky.

We could see the angry black skies growing angrier by the minute. The wind felt like it was blowing toward the storm, which led thousands of people around Jordan-Hare Stadium to have the following conversation simultaneously.

"Well, the wind is blowing *away* from us."

"That's great, but you see the storm is still coming *toward* us."

There were hopeful souls, myself included, who kept saying aloud that the storm was obviously going to drift just south of us. But when the public address announcer informed everyone that lightning was in the area, and the stadium needed to be evacuated immediately, all hope was abandoned.

Logistically it is nearly impossible to move 87,000 people from one place to another in a very short period of time, especially when you are trying to move them to no place in particular. We were just told to leave the stadium, which for some meant the lower concourse, for others their tailgates, and others may still be running to this very day. For the first people out, it meant lining the exit tunnels, thus making it even harder to evacuate. Within a matter of minutes we were logjammed, and then the rain came.

I lived on the Gulf Coast for four years, and what blew through Auburn that night was a tropical storm in everything but name.[5] Sheets of stinging rain slapped our faces at thirty miles an hour. Within seconds we were as wet as we could possibly be, despite the best efforts of our three-dollar ponchos. All the while lightning was crashing around Auburn. I'll admit it, I was a little scared.

It took us close to half an hour to make our way out of the stadium and down to the concourse, where we wedged ourselves into the mass of angry, waterlogged college football fans. A scuffle broke out between two grown men just to my left, and I began to hyperventilate, anticipating a soccer-style fan stampede. We had devolved from peaceful football crowd to Thunderdome in half an hour. My flight response took over, and I began pushing my way through the crowd for the safety of the thunderstorm. It wasn't until I was again standing in the driving rain that I realized I'd left Tricia and Jordan inside.

---

5. Actually, we can change that right now. How about Tropical Storm Chizik? Someone call Jim Cantore.

Fortunately they had been following me, and we huddled under an awning across the street with a few other refugees. Inside we could hear the Auburn student section, who, to a person, kept their seats during the entire rain event. They belted out the words to Creedence Clearwater Revival's "Have You Ever Seen the Rain," followed by "Who'll Stop the Rain," and then any other rain-inspired song the press box could find to play. Then we heard an eruption of cheers, and we knew football was finally going to be played.

We waited for the concourse to clear before swimming back to the stadium. The field looked incredible despite the amount of rain it took on. In contrast, everyone around me looked miserable, especially after the wind kicked up and turned a wet night into a cold wet night. This was about the time I realized the eagle would not be flying.

Since the late nineties Auburn has been flying a live golden eagle before games. It is let loose from a cage high above the stadium, and it circles the field a few times before landing, on cue, at the fifty-yard line. It is, without a doubt, the coolest thing ever. Now Jordan was going to miss it, in part because the wind was blowing too hard, but mostly because we were well over an hour past the scheduled kickoff, and if we wanted to finish the game before Monday, we needed to get things going. Sadly we would also miss the Auburn University Marching Band's pregame show, an electrifying display of high-stepping ridiculousness. The players just ran out of the tunnel and we started the game. Very minimalist. Like letting a Primitive Baptist run your pregame.

The game started with little fanfare, and then West Virginia scored on their fifth play of the game. We generously gave them the ball back, and their running back, Noel Devine, who is roughly the size of a squirrel, ran seventy-one yards for another touchdown.

Through the years, Tricia and I have only left one Auburn game early, a 2003 game in Baton Rouge that I'll tell you more about later. We thought about leaving a few times this night. Tricia, who is a medical resident, had to be at work by 6:00 the next morning for a thirty-hour shift. We were already going to get home late, but with the ninety-minute delay we wouldn't be in bed before 2:00 a.m.

But Auburn finally kicked a field goal, then scooped up a fumble, and somehow cut the lead to 21–20 at halftime. The Tigers left the field to boisterous applause, and throughout the break you could sense a growing excitement in Jordan-Hare. The kind of excitement you get when you know your team has a chance to do something special, not the kind you get when lightning is crashing a few yards away.

The second half was full of big plays, and about midway through the fourth quarter Chris Todd hit Darvin Adams on a seventeen-yard touchdown pass to take a 34–30 lead. No one was breathing though, because Auburn had given up too many big plays that night to relax just yet. Then it happened. With about four minutes to go, and with WVU deep in their own territory, a pass was deflected up in the air, and Auburn linebacker Craig Stephens corralled it and rumbled fifteen yards for the score.

Jordan-Hare Stadium went feral. Old women broke into impromptu dances, grown men embraced complete strangers, and children were thrown into the air as sacrifices to whatever god let this happen. Tricia and I hugged and jumped simultaneously, then turned to see Jordan Green high-fiving everyone in the row behind us.[6] We cheered until the last player had left the field, then took Jordan back to Toomer's Corner to participate in the rolling. Since soggy toilet paper doesn't unroll very well, people were basically

---

6. Later that night at the tailgate, my friend J. T. told me our friend Charles turned to him during the celebration and yelled, "Do you think this is what heaven will feel like?"

just throwing big globs of wet toilet paper that stuck to whatever they hit. Usually Toomer's looks like a winter wonderland, but tonight it looked more like a plumbing disaster. Even so, it was the most beautiful backed-up toilet I'd ever seen.

We made it back to Birmingham about 3:00 a.m. Tricia slept for three hours and went to work. Jordan and I slept much later, then spent most of Sunday rehashing everything we could remember from the game. When I put him on a plane to Phoenix the next day, I knew I'd done my part. Now I just had to sit back and let the spirit move.

● ● ●

A few weeks later, I called Jordan to follow up like the overaggressive evangelical I am. We talked about the year, his trip to Auburn, and then he went on and on about how his Oregon Ducks were destined for the Rose Bowl. I was crushed.

"So," I conceded, "I guess you didn't become an Auburn fan after your trip."

"Well," Jordan said sheepishly, "I cheer for you guys, but if Oregon needed Auburn to lose, well, I'd want you to lose."

The call went awkwardly quiet as neither of us knew what to say, but finally Jordan tried, "I mean, it was awesome, the whole SEC thing. I can tell how much football means to you guys. It's obviously very important. But I don't think I would want that, you know? It just wouldn't be as fun if every game had the potential to ruin my life."

"I guess not," I said, feeling like an idiot. It pained me that I'd spent so much time trying to pull Jordan into the same mess that I struggle with daily, the same mess I've pulled countless others into. I'm a Christian. I claim to be in the most important relationship in the world—the one with my creator, Jesus Christ—and yet I tell others about the Tigers a hundred times more often. Perhaps it's time I realize that the Auburn family, as special as it is, is not the most important thing I can tell people about.

You know, I truly am thankful for all God has done for me, including letting me go to Auburn.

Sometimes I just have an odd way of showing it.

WEEK 3

UNIVERSITY OF SOUTH CAROLINA

SEPTEMBER 24, 2009

Five days shalt thou labour, as the Bible says. The seventh is the Lord thy God's. The sixth day is for football.

Anthony Burgess

SINCE THE BEGINNING OF TIME, humans have used the days of the week as a scheduling guide.

Sundays are for keeping holy and dreading Mondays. Mondays are for complaining that Saturday and Sunday seemed shorter than they actually were. Tuesdays are for elections and stock market crashes. Wednesdays are for going to church, even though the Bible doesn't say you have to. Thursdays are for Thanksgiving and wishing it were Friday. Fridays are for wearing blue jeans to work and going to see Meg Ryan movies with persons of the opposite sex. Saturdays are for mowing grass and attending college football games.

This simple method worked for millennia, until some genius at the NCAA decided to start playing college football games on Thursday night.

Thursday night football is, in a word, unnatural. It's like Christmas in March, or shrimp scampi for breakfast, or Billy Graham at Hooters. Thursday night football is, in my humble opinion, an affront to God Almighty. And it's why, on Saturday, September 26, I found myself at the Midtown Seventh-Day Adventist Church in Columbia, South Carolina, instead of down the street at Williams-Brice Stadium.

Before this week my experience with Seventh-Day Adventists had been limited to one encounter. During my senior year in college, I worked part time for a great company near Auburn and had hoped to parlay the experience into a full-time job. One afternoon the CEO called me into his office, and I sat down across from him, full of hope. But instead of praising my work ethic and discussing my future with his company, he informed me, over the course of an hour, why I should go to church on Saturday.

I've forgotten most of what he told me that day, but I remember he talked a lot about Constantine, the Roman Emperor who decided back in the day to move the Roman day of rest from Saturday to Sunday. This apparently led to some confusion among believers, who then started keeping the wrong day holy. Since then God has been pretty upset with the majority of us.

At Midtown that morning, no one mentioned how angry God would be if we didn't keep Saturday holy. Of course, everyone there *was* keeping Saturday holy, so it would have been preaching to the choir, even though Midtown doesn't actually have a choir.

At the time, Midtown met in a large ballroom at a senior center in — you guessed it — midtown Columbia. I showed up way too early, so I sat in the parking lot and watched as church members sporadically arrived. This was nice because it gave me a chance to look for crazies. But everyone who showed up looked at least as normal as me, so I followed their lead and went inside.

With only fifty people in attendance, I was *way* too easy to spot. I probably shook the hand of every person in the church and had the following conversation at least five times.

"We're so glad to have you with us today."

"Thank you. I'm glad to be here."

"Do you live here in Columbia?"

"No, I actually live in Birmingham."

"Oh, are you here on business?"

"No, I'm not."

"Are you thinking of moving to Columbia?"

"Not really."

"So you're here seeing family in Columbia?"

"No, I'm just visiting your church."

This would usually garner an odd look and bring an abrupt end to the conversation. I hated to be dishonest, since technically I was in town on business, but if I told them why, they'd know I was technically working as we spoke, on what technically they consider the Sabbath. Besides, I would've hated to have been asked to leave on what amounts to a technicality.

Once I had met everyone, the service began, and soon I forgot I was even at an SDA church. A lady played piano while another led us in some hymns from a hymnal that looked eerily similar to the hymnals at my home church. I flipped through the pages during a prayer and didn't see a single mention of Constantine.

At Dawson Memorial Baptist Church back in Birmingham, as with many other large churches I've attended, visitors are all welcomed in one fell swoop. This is done, we are told, so as not to embarrass anyone. Every time I sit through this, I wonder if there is a church out there that actually does embarrass visitors.

It turns out there is.

When Pastor Walter Fry stood to greet us, he began scanning the room, searching frantically for an unfamiliar face. I slumped down a bit, but the woman in front of me began grunting and motioning in my direction until she caught Pastor Fry's attention. "Yes," he said. "Our brother in the back there. Please tell us your name."

I stood up with every eye in Midtown focused on me and said, "My name is Chad Gibbs. I'm visiting from Birmingham."

"Brother Chad, are you looking to move to Columbia?"

"No, sir."

"Well, we wish you would."

This was accompanied by a few amens from around the room. I'd never been amened before, and it felt good. I began to wonder if perhaps I *should* move to Columbia.

After that my morning at Midtown was largely uneventful, though two things stood out: the first was the lack of teenagers and college kids, although that demographic would probably be the toughest to sell on the whole sundown Friday to sundown Saturday thing. The second was that I did not hear a soul in the congregation mention college football. This was particularly odd in light of what had happened two days earlier at Williams-Brice Stadium.

● ● ●

When I was scheduling my way through a season of SEC football, I had no idea that South Carolina and Ole Miss would be playing on a Thursday night. Had I known, I would have certainly picked another week to visit, since a weeknight game meant that if I stayed for church on Sunday, I'd be in a foreign town four consecutive days, and I'd be required by law to add a state flag decal to my car.

The University of South Carolina is located in the state capital of Columbia. I wasn't even sure how far Columbia was from Birmingham but was pleased to learn it was only a five-and-a-half-hour drive. I wasn't pleased when I realized, somewhere near Augusta, that I had zero cash, no ATM card, and no ticket to the game. Nabbing a scalped ticket without cash would be difficult without a pistol and ski mask, so I looked around the car for something I could barter with. All I had with me were some old golf spikes and twenty bottles of water that had been in my trunk for at least three years.

That's when I remembered that I could use my smartphone to connect with the ticket office of the University of South Carolina and purchase a ticket for that day's game, all from the comfort of my recklessly swerving vehicle. We live in wonderful times indeed.

After a quick lunch at Groucho's Deli, I made my way to Jack Haynes's house just outside of Columbia. Mark Wegner and Jimmy Easterby of First Presbyterian Church put me in touch with Mr. Haynes. They told me there was not a greater Gamecock fan. They told me the truth.

I had spoken to Mr. Haynes earlier that week by phone, and he asked if I planned to ride with him to the game. I said I could, and he replied, "Good, you *want* to ride to the game with me." This was a little cryptic, but Mr. Haynes wouldn't elaborate. Needless to say, I was a tad apprehensive when I pulled into his quiet suburban neighborhood.

There wasn't much doubt which house was Jack Haynes's. It was the one with the garnet and black 1964 Ford Econoline van sitting out front. The van was covered with more Gamecock stickers and magnets than you could dream, and each window was host to at least two USC car flags. Mr. Haynes was loading it down with tailgate supplies when I pulled up.

We shook hands, and Mr. Haynes gave me a quick history of the van, including how much he purchased it for ($1 from his father), and which opposing fans had scraped paint off with their keys. Then he took me inside to meet his wife, Bonnie.

Mrs. Haynes was putting the finishing touches on the evening's meal and began handing us covered dishes to load in the van. Once back inside, she handed me a one-page bio of Mr. Haynes she'd put together when nominating him for the Legendary Gamecock Fan contest. The numbers were mind-boggling.

Jack Haynes went to his first University of South Carolina football game at the age of eight. He would not miss a home game until he was thirty-six. That's twenty-eight consecutive years. He is now sixty-three, retired, and in the last fifty-five seasons has only missed five USC home games. Did you catch that? He's only missed five home games in the last fifty-five seasons! There are head coaches that have missed more of their team's games.

The numbers kept piling up. Mr. Haynes has gone to fifty-five consecutive South Carolina–Clemson games. He has never left a game early. And he has only missed sixteen home basketball games in the last forty-five years.

I'd always heard South Carolina had some of the most loyal and dedicated fans in the country, and after talking to just one of them I believed it. Only twenty-five of those fifty-five seasons were winning seasons, so Jack wasn't jumping on the bandwagon of some national powerhouse. Of the fifty-five consecutive Clemson–USC games Jack attended, USC lost two-thirds. Mr. Haynes loves the Gamecocks simply because they are the Gamecocks.

I began to realize Mr. Haynes was living my dream life. Ever since I left Auburn, I've wanted to move back. We'd buy season tickets to every sport and never miss a minute of the action. And that is pretty weird when you think about it. I'm thirty-one, with most of my adult life ahead of me, and I dream of living in a small Alabama town and letting my life revolve around college athletics. Sure, sometimes I read about Christians doing great things all over the globe and think that could be me, but my thoughts always drift back to Auburn. And truthfully, I'm not even sure I could handle living there, at least not as well as Jack Haynes handles Columbia. He is an elder at First Presbyterian, and he has a large role on the pastoral care team, visiting the sick and elderly in the church. Could I possibly be so balanced if I lived five minutes from Jordan-Hare Stadium? I honestly don't know. Perhaps living in Auburn would help me see the game for what it is—a game. But then again, I can totally see me sneaking around the shrubs of the practice field, trying to learn the trick plays in advance.

I don't think God would let me live in a town like Auburn and not want me to enjoy football. That seems cruel and unusual. I guess I still haven't quite figured out what God wants, which is my real problem.

Once the van was loaded down with enough food to feed a small country, we got on the road. Being the guest, I was given the privilege of riding shotgun. This was great until I realized the van was not equipped with safety belts. When we hit the interstate, I began to have trouble breathing. Jack Haynes is no spring chicken. My mind kept dreaming up nightmare scenarios in which he had a heart attack or fell asleep at the wheel, sending us, unrestrained, into oncoming traffic. To make matters worse, the van's speedometer said we were going 110 mph. (We *were* being passed right and left by honking cars, so I suppose the gauge *could* have been broken.)

Thankfully we made it off the interstate and into the South Carolina State Fairgrounds and State Farmers' Market, where Williams-Brice Stadium is located. Mr. Haynes popped a beat-up old cassette tape into his stereo, the speakers crackled for a few seconds, then bystanders leaped as the sound of a rooster's crow blared from two massive speakers concealed in the van's front grill. This was followed by more rooster crows along with some songs and cheers. Now people were clapping along to the music and high-fiving Mr. Haynes and me as the van crept through a combination of game-day and Thursday rush-hour traffic.

The Hayneses have been members of the Gamecock Club for forty years, which means they have a sweet parking spot on game days. We stopped no more than a long field goal from the stadium and set up our makeshift banquet. BBQ chicken was on the menu, which seemed a little cannibalistic for USC fans but was delicious nonetheless. There was also a hodgepodge of chips, dips, and sweets, and I tried them all with complete disregard to my waistline.

Between bites I asked Mr. Haynes if he thought the Gamecocks had a shot that night versus the fourth-ranked Ole Miss Rebels. "They are number four in the country," Mr. Haynes said. "But we are only a three-point underdog. I think people know something big might happen tonight." And with that I swear his eyes twinkled.

Heading out to see some other folks before kickoff, I made my way through the USC tailgates in the enormous parking lot located just across George Rogers Boulevard from the stadium. This is where I found Devin Olenick and the rest of Campus Advance, the college ministry of the Columbia Church of Christ.

Devin and some guys were, shockingly, playing cornhole when I walked up. I watched for a minute, but cornhole is not a very spectator-friendly sport, so I started asking Devin about his story, which sounded familiar. We talked about how upset we get when our team loses, even though we have no control over the game, and, unless we are dumb enough to have gambled on the outcome, really are not affected in any way whatsoever. "I've been furious over losses for an entire night," he told me. "I've even let it affect my relationships. But I think I'm getting better." The last part was pretty universal in my conversations this fall. Everyone thinks he is getting better.

But are we really getting better? I think sometimes we confuse getting older with getting better. We learn it's socially awkward to sit in the corner and pout for an entire weekend,[1] but if we are still pouting in our minds, does that make it any better? How is your prayer life when you've spent the last day inwardly sulking? I know how mine is—lousy.

Sure, I'm getting better. I'm getting better at not letting you know how much an Auburn loss truly hurts me.

• • •

Kickoff was rapidly approaching, so I stopped by will-call and picked up my ticket. The seat was pretty decent—thirty-yard line, about thirty rows up—but when I sat down, I realized I was bisecting a family of four.

"Yeah, for some reason our season tickets had a one-seat gap in them, and each week someone new sits between us."

"That's fun," I said.

"Not really," they replied, so I moved over and let them reunite.

Before the University of South Carolina Marching Band took the field for its pregame show, Tim Stewart, director of the USC Baptist Collegiate Ministry, led the stadium in prayer. I had not heard a football game start with a prayer since 1996, my senior year of high school, and that prayer was led by me.

Each week at Glencoe High School, a senior had been asked to give the invocation before the game. We were now in the playoffs, and apparently they'd run out of people to ask, so they came to me. I led the stadium in prayer, then watched as rain and forty-mile-per-hour winds ripped umbrellas from the hands of screaming fans and threw them (the umbrellas, not the fans) hundreds of feet in the air. Glencoe won the game, which I took sole credit for, though the thunderstorm was much more likely my doing.

Thankfully for everyone in attendance, Tim Stewart's prayer did not invoke the wrath of God, and the band took the field on

1. Unless you are spectacularly drunk, which seems to make it more acceptable.

a gorgeous September night, marching up and down playing circus music.[2] People around me kept making these weird C-shaped signs with their hands, which I guess stood for Carolina, but I never found out for sure. Finally the band marched down toward the players' entrance, forming a human tunnel, and the stadium became eerily silent.

South Carolina's pregame entrance has been voted the best in the nation by people who have time to vote on such things. I'm not certain it is the best, but it has to be the most dramatic. The stadium takes a collective breath and is brought to life by what sounds like a twelve-ton rooster crowing in the distance. Then come the first notes of the theme from *2001: A Space Odyssey*. Bum, Bum, Bum … BUM BUM!!! While the crowd is working itself into a cock-a-doodle frenzy, a black curtain is pulled from a cage at midfield, revealing Cocky, USC's six-foot rooster mascot, running around like decapitated poultry is apt to do. And just as the song reaches its crescendo, the team rushes onto the field to the thunderous applause of 80,250 of the most dedicated fans in America. Seeing this alone would've been worth the price of admission.

Ole Miss entered the game ranked number four in the nation. This seemed like a bit of a stretch to most people, but I suppose someone had to be ranked number four. At first the game was, well, pretty boring actually. South Carolina managed to kick two first-half field goals, held Ole Miss to only one, and led halfway, 6–3.

Early in the second half, USC settled on a field goal after quarterback Stephen Garcia followed a sixty-nine-yard pass by taking

---

2. Okay, that is not entirely true. They were probably playing the South Carolina fight song. But as a general rule most SEC fans think their fight song alone can invoke misty-eyed fervor, while all the others sound like music clowns should juggle to.

a bad sack and throwing an ugly incompletion. Steve Spurrier was now destroying his visor, though his team held a six-point lead over a Top 5 team. But then Ole Miss fumbled, and Garcia made a great play with his legs, then a perfect pass to Patrick DiMarco for a two-yard touchdown. It was 16–3, South Carolina, and Williams-Brice Stadium was reaching all-new levels of hysteria. Students were dancing, Cocky was dancing, alumni young and old were dancing, and—I'll admit it—even I was channeling my inner MC Hammer. Everyone knew the score would hold.

Everyone, that is, except the man in front of me, a guy named Tony, who still looked like his lunch would soon be making a reappearance. When Ole Miss hit a fifty-yard touchdown pass with ten minutes to play, everyone suddenly looked a lot like Tony. The guy next to me began taking pulls from the flask he had snuck in, preparing himself for what everyone seemed to think was now inevitable. Ole Miss got the ball back with four minutes left, and with one big play they were down to the South Carolina thirty-two-yard line, only a touchdown and extra point away from sending everyone home unhappy.

But the Gamecocks got a stop on first down, followed by a stop on second down, and on third down Ole Miss quarterback Javon Sneed was sacked for a big loss. It was fourth down and nineteen. The Gamecocks were one stop away from the biggest home win in school history. Sneed dropped back to pass and fired toward a receiver on the sideline, but the pass was tipped away and fell harmlessly to the turf. The reaction seemed delayed. I think USC fans were searching for a pass-interference flag they just knew was coming, but there were no flags. Rave music once again filled the Columbia night, and I hugged and danced with complete strangers as we celebrated the monumental win. Cock-a-doodle-doo.

I took my time walking back. Many of the tailgates I passed now looked like miniature versions of Williams-Brice, complete with music, cheering, and at least one live rooster. Some were already watching the replay of the game, and I got the feeling they were going to watch the entire thing again before they packed up to leave. When I finally made it back to Mr. Haynes's van, he was grinning like Clemson had just been placed on probation. We loaded up and hit the road, blasting the theme from *2001* and high-fiving everyone we passed.

"You know," I confessed to Mr. Haynes. "I feel a little guilty that you've been coming to games for fifty-five years, and I show up for just one and see the biggest home win in school history."

"Oh, don't feel guilty," Mr. Haynes said. "Just come back every week from now on."

● ● ●

Driving home from Columbia, I thought a lot about devotion. What else would keep USC fans coming back year after year, even though they'd never seen their Gamecocks beat a Top 5 team at home? I think most of us find this kind of loyalty admirable, but maybe we shouldn't. I don't mean this as a criticism of Mr. Haynes — after hearing about all he does in his church, I've decided he is one of those rare individuals who seems to have forty-eight hours in a day. I'm talking about myself and what kind of life I'm going to live once this journey is over. Most likely my wife and I will have the money and time to attend every Auburn football game from now until Judgment Day. But should we? I'm already concerned my devotion to all things Auburn has skewed my priorities, and we should miss a game or two each season.

So what do I think God wants? Well, I think the Sunday school answer is he wants a relationship with me, but more than that, he wants an honest relationship with me. It's nice to think time will make us better Christians. That just by waking up each morning, we're becoming the men and women God has called us to be, but I'm afraid time just makes us better fakers. We learn the buzzwords. We learn what we can get away with. But that doesn't mean we are growing. These are the kinds of lukewarm relationships God talks about spewing out of his mouth.

God wants me to know him, and he wants to know me, the real me. And who is the real me? Well, the real me is a lukewarm Christian who still places way too much importance on football. Sure, others may not realize it, but like I said earlier, I don't handle losses any better; I just handle them differently, more privately. The image I've crafted is so good that at times I fool myself, but when I'm honest, I don't really like who I'm becoming. I know to the world it doesn't look so bad, because I'm not committing atrocities against mankind. I'm just another person who really loves football, someone who doesn't let anything keep him from watching the game. But maybe, just maybe, I should leave open the possibility that occasionally God has other plans for my Saturdays, because when I'm on my deathbed, I doubt I'll look back and say, "You know, I wish I had gone to more college football games."

UNIVERSITY OF TENNESSEE

OCTOBER 3, 2009

I find your lack of faith disturbing.

Darth Vader

WITH **783** WINS, the Tennessee Volunteers are the ninth-winningest football program in NCAA Division I history. They've won twenty-five bowl games, thirteen Southeastern Conference titles, and stake claim to six national championships. Their home games are played at Neyland Stadium, a structure so large it can hold 109,000 people and Lane Kiffin's ego. Football is very important in Tennessee, and most years Tennessee is very good at football. Two thousand eight, however, was not most years.

The season started off with an overtime loss to UCLA, followed by losses to Florida and Auburn. After an embarrassing loss to South Carolina that ran the Vols' record to 3–6, Phillip Fulmer, Tennessee's coach for the past sixteen seasons, announced he would resign at the end of the season. The team was so inspired by this that they lost their homecoming game to Wyoming, thus eliminating any hope of a bowl game. The season mercifully ended with a 28–10 win over Kentucky, and coach Fulmer was carried off the field and promptly thrown to the curb.

Fast-forward ten months and the masses were still a little depressed. My dozens of emails to Knoxville area churches and UT campus ministries had yielded exactly zero people who admitted to being Christians and rabid Volunteers fans. This was shocking since *USA Today* ranked Tennessee as the country's fourth most religious state, and all but fifteen people in Tennessee are rabid Vols fans.[1] Clearly, the residents of the Volunteer State were suffering from a lack of faith. We all experience this at one time or another. A loved one dies or you lose your homecoming game to Wyoming, and all of a sudden everything that was good and certain in the world now seems random and indifferent at best. Auburn fans can relate, since our 2008 record was identical to Tennessee's, and we too fired an occasionally beloved longtime coach. But that is where the similarities end. Auburn hired Gene Chizik, the Iowa State head coach with a lifetime record of 5–19, sending its fans into deeper depression. Tennessee made more of a splash in hiring Lane Kiffin, the football equivalent of Zack Morris, leading Vols fans to believe a league title was just around the corner. But Chizik proved a hard worker who hired an even harder-working staff, while Kiffin spent most of the summer making public apologies for saying everything he thought out loud. Consequently Auburn was off to a 4–0 start, while the Vols were 2–2 and didn't really want to talk about it.

But the week before the game, I finally spoke with UT student Chris Sells, who is an active member in a student organization called Volunteers for Christ, and he and his friends agreed to meet

---

1. For a complete list of Tennessee citizens who are not rabid Vols fans, see appendix I.

Tricia and me for dinner. (Tricia was still bitter she missed the 2004 Auburn–Tennessee game and wasn't about to miss this one.) We told them to pick the place but suggested something local. They picked Chili's.

We met up with Chris and his friends Nathan Simmons and Diggity[2] outside of the Knoxville Chili's. Chris was a fresh-faced college kid in a strange T-shirt, sporting a disco-era afro. Nathan was a fifth-year engineering student with the kind of beard birds could nest in. And Diggity looked about fifteen years old and was wearing his hat at what I considered a preposterous angle on his head. The five of us ordered chicken finger platters, and Chris began to tell us about their organization.

Volunteers for Christ, or VFC, isn't really a volunteer organization, at least not in the sense that they will rake your leaves for free. They obviously volunteer to do *some* stuff, like eat dinner with strange writers, but they use *volunteer* as a play on Tennessee's mascot.[3] VFC is the student ministry of Cornerstone Church of Knoxville. Cornerstone is nondenominational and associated with Sovereign Grace Ministries. I'd never heard of Sovereign Grace Ministries, which would prove embarrassing.

"So what's your other book about?" one of the guys asked, referring to the first book I wrote.

"It's a collection of humorous essays," I told them, then tried to think of an essay these three guys would appreciate. "Have you heard of the Joshua Harris book *I Kissed Dating Goodbye?*"

I'd written a chapter on Harris called *I Kissed Dating Goodbye, With My Tongue*, in which I basically blame Harris's courtship manifesto for my lifetime of dating woes. A lot of guys I've told

---

2. Diggity, I'm almost certain, is not his given name. But I never learned it, so I'll assume he is just a one-name guy like Prince or Fabio.
3. At least it's not called Cats for Christ. Oh, wait; that's Kentucky. For some reason, I giggle every time I think about it.

this to think it's funny, and we laugh and spend a few minutes Harris bashing. It's all very Christlike.

"Yes! That book is great. Joshua Harris is on the leadership team at Sovereign Grace."

"Oh," I said.

"Why?" they asked.

"No reason," I said. "Just wondering if you'd heard of it."

I thought it best to change the subject and steered the conversation toward football. Diggity had grown up all over the country and never really had a team of his own until he got to college. Nathan was originally from Memphis and had some Ole Miss leanings, but now he bled orange. And Chris, who grew up in Chattanooga, actually played for the Vols in 2007, or so he said. "I walked on in 2007, went through spring practice the next year, then didn't make the team in 2008." Chris didn't seem like a pathological liar, but I never believe anyone smaller than me when he says he played Division I sports. So when I got home, I consulted the Internet and, sure enough, either Chris stole a uniform and convinced the team to act like they knew him, or he really was a Vol for a year.

Tricia and I told them about our time at Auburn and reminisced about how much we enjoyed our college days. Then one of them asked me, in all seriousness, "Were you in school at the same time as Bo Jackson?"

Bo Jackson's senior season at Auburn was 1985, the same year I entered the first grade. Either these guys weren't too keen on SEC history, or my hair was graying faster than I realized.

After dinner the guys volunteered to give us a tour of UT's campus. It is, to put it mildly, hilly. And I know it's unfair to judge the aesthetics of a campus while walking through it at night, but the parts we saw were not the prettiest I've encountered. Seems Tennessee had the misfortune of conducting a lot of building campaigns in the early 1970s.

Tricia, always the diplomat, told them, "This is a very pretty campus."

They sighed audibly. "Don't patronize us. The *Princeton Review* ranks it one of the nation's least beautiful campuses every year."[4]

"Yeah," Tricia conceded, while I wondered aloud why someone would actually rank ugly campuses.

Our tour weaved in and out of buildings and up and down hills, eventually leading us by Gibbs Hall, an athletic dorm named, I suppose, in honor of my visit. Then we took the main concourse back through campus and stumbled upon what looked like a giant sunflower being sucked into an upside-down tornado. This was a sculpture named, and I'm not making this up, "A Startling Whirlwind of Opportunity." It had been installed over the summer while most students were out of town, and once they returned I'm sure they were startled. I hear there are plans to cover it with a tarp next time the *Princeton Review* comes to town.

The next morning we woke up early and made our way back to campus. The guys from Volunteers for Christ said we could park at their place, which was fortunate, since most Christian organizations use game-day parking as a source of revenue. As we pulled in, Nathan Simmons walked out to greet us, then offered a tour of the house.

Walking into the kitchen, a couple of guys were standing around drinking coffee and talking to a girl named Adair Poschel. I mention this only because Adair Poschel is a cool name. The downstairs den was spacious and had enough couches and chairs to accommodate most of Knoxville. Upstairs were the clean and tidy bedrooms, which included shelves lined with Joshua Harris books.

"This is the master bathroom," Nathan told us. "It has heated floors."

---

4. UT–Knoxville is ranked twelfth on the *Princeton Review*'s Least Beautiful Campus list. The New Jersey Institute of Technology holds the top spot.

It took a few seconds for this to register. "Wait," I said. "Your bathroom has heated floors? Did one of you win Powerball?"

In college I was lucky to have heated water in my bathroom, let alone heated floors. One year my bathroom didn't even have a door. I asked Nathan if I could take a shower. He politely refused.

● ● ●

We left the VFC house around 10:00 a.m. and headed over to Neyland Stadium, which is perched on the banks of the Tennessee River. This is where we discovered perhaps the most awesome college football tradition ever involving pontoon boats. The Volunteer Navy began in 1962 when Tennessee broadcaster George Mooney decided to avoid traffic and drive his boat to the game. Now more than 200 boats dock just outside the stadium. On any given Saturday you are likely to see a million-dollar yacht anchored next to some guys who floated in on logs. I suppose Auburn fans could wade to the game down Saugahatchee Creek, but it just wouldn't be the same.

The river was home to a handful of restaurants, and we picked a place called Calhoun's for lunch. We ordered burgers and began watching the Alabama–Kentucky game on one of Calhoun's forty televisions. The first half was almost over, but the Tide only led 7–6, and when Kentucky's punter pinned Alabama inside its own one-yard line, I expected Calhoun's to erupt, but hardly anyone said a word. The UT fans around us just kept eating their hickory-smoked BBQ like nothing happened. What was going on? Were Tennessee fans so depressed they couldn't be bothered to applaud the misfortunes of their most detested adversary? I asked Tricia if she could prescribe the entire restaurant something for depression. Minutes later, when the Tide completed their ninety-nine-yard touchdown drive, a Vols fan across the room actually clapped. Somewhere beyond this world, without really knowing why, General Robert Neyland began to weep.

"Perhaps the Tennessee fans have just learned to balance their faith with their fanaticism," Tricia said, mocking both them and me.

"No," I said. "This isn't Pentecost. A hundred thousand people don't just change all at once. They're just depressed because they're losing, and now they're not sure they hired the right coach. They'll be back." I'd already learned this from experience. Sure, the depression from losing makes you feel like you don't care as much, but it's really more of a general apathy toward life. One big win and you are as messed up as ever.

After lunch we contemplated trying to sink the inflatable portions of the Vol Navy with some sharp sticks, but we decided instead to head back to Neyland Stadium and meet David Wells, another guy from VFC, who also worked for the school paper as an aspiring member of the press.[5] I liked David immediately, especially after hearing his careful exegesis of Tim Tebow's eye-black verses. "I'm all for John 3:16," David said. "But I feel like using Philippians 4:13 at a football game is taking things a little out of context. People are looking up these verses, and when they read the one from Philippians, I fear they'll think Tebow believes he won the Heisman because God is Gator fan."

At the time I thought David was putting too much thought into things, but as the season wore on, I met person after person who believed, in all sincerity, that God was in fact showing Tebow preferential treatment. Though it's hard to say if this was based more on his eye-black or the mounting evidence that God *was* showing Tim preferential treatment.

We went on to talk about our common struggles, and then David confided, "I often depend on football rather than Christ

---

5. At a press conference the year before, David had the pleasure of being yelled at by Coach Fulmer for asking a question he had already answered. It made me think of press conferences as a high-stakes game of memory, where the losers get humiliated, and the winners get boring answers.

for happiness. The spectacle is so enticing, and it is immediately more gratifying."

David had hit on something with his immediate gratification comment. Football can take your emotions from zero to awesome in 4.2 seconds. When I'm there, in the stadium, it all feels so important, and when the big play comes, I am screaming and leaping around. I raise my arms in the air and sing with all my might. The feeling can last for weeks if the win is big enough. The flip side is the immediate despair a loss can bring, and that feeling can last for weeks as well. And maybe that is the problem, because both wins and losses have an effect on the way I worship the following day. When Auburn wins, I can't wait to put on my orange and blue tie and go to church. But after a loss, the morning's worship feels covered in a veil of gloom. So maybe the question is, why does the result of a football game have any bearing on how I worship the God of the universe?

David had to get to work for the school paper, so we went to see Victor Thompson, a retired music minister who tailgates in the shadows of Neyland Stadium, overlooking the Tennessee River. Mr. Thompson took us around, introducing us to every member of his massive tailgate. More than once I heard someone say, "This is what football season is all about," meaning gathering outdoors on a beautiful fall day with friends and family. Maybe they are right, but if Auburn were to lose on any given day, I'd just as soon be at the bottom of the river than with friends and family.

Eva Thompson, Victor's wife, told us about his last Sunday as the music minister for First United Methodist Church in Morristown, Tennessee. "We were emotional already," she said, "and to close the service the organist played one of Victor's favorite hymns. But it sounded strange—you could see people looking around. Then we realized she was playing 'Rocky Top' with her foot pedals."

Mr. Thompson was smiling. "We hardly missed a game," he said. "But when I was on staff at Trinity UMC in Huntsville, the night games were rough. Sometimes we wouldn't leave Knoxville until well after midnight, and by the time we got back to Huntsville, I'd just shower off and head in to church for our Sunday morning staff meetings."

I wondered later what to think of the all-nighters Mr. Thompson used to pull to see his Vols play. I'll admit my first reaction was judgmental. *He was putting God and his job second to his love for football. No way he was giving his all to the church if he was leading worship without any sleep.* But who am I to say that? Maybe he can operate without sleep; my wife can. Or maybe those Saturdays in the fall were the best time to get the entire family together, like they were this Saturday.

I like black and white. I like a formulaic approach to life, particularly my Christianity, but it's not always that easy. I just said what I think God wants from us is a relationship, and who am I to judge Mr. Thompson's relationship with God? But you know what? Maybe part of the reason I started making these trips was to find people who I thought were worse than me, so I could feel better about myself. It's probably the reason I wanted to evangelize Jordan Green, because the more rabid fans I can make, the better I can feel about myself. And that is part of my problem, because going to a football game and enjoying yourself is not an affront to God, and not everyone I see at a game is there because he needs a win to fill some void in his life. The questions I'm working on are between God and me, and I certainly won't find the answers by judging others.

● ● ●

Finding our seats in Neyland Stadium proved difficult without a Sherpa to guide us. From the outside, Neyland does not appear *that* big, but once inside we were overwhelmed. Where most stadiums have an upper deck or two, Tennessee has a singular upper deck that wraps around the entire stadium. I'm surprised that during construction God didn't make the workers start talking in different languages. And once 100,000 people file in and start screaming the words to "Rocky Top," well, you start to wonder if perhaps you should have stayed at home.

The night started off well for the Tigers, who, after watching a three-minute rap video[6] promoting Tennessee safety Eric Berry for the Heisman Trophy, jumped out to a 13–0 lead on the home team. This was Auburn's season in a nutshell. Early in games I'd think I was watching a magic show. Reverses, halfback passes, and whatever craziness Gus Malzahn, Auburn's mad scientist of an OC, could concoct. But Auburn never really kept its foot on the pedal for an entire game, and just before the half UT put a touchdown on the board to cut the lead to 13–6, thus waking Neyland Stadium from the dead.

The second half was almost a mirror image of the first. Auburn put ten points on the board and led by three scores with less than thirteen minutes to play. Fans began to file out of the stadium, but Tennessee continued to play hard, scoring a quick ten points and pulling to within a touchdown. But Auburn drove down the field and added a field goal when they had to, all but sealing the hard-fought victory. Those in bright orange started the long journey to their cars, while we in burnt orange serenaded our undefeated Tigers back to their locker room. And after posing for victory photos in front of Neyland's massive scoreboard, we walked victorious into the cool Knoxville night.

Back at the VFC house, about ten guys were sitting in the garage, which had been remodeled into a spectacular home theater.

---

6. The song had the regrettable quality of being both awful and catchy, causing me to sing it the rest of the night. Eric Berryyyyy, Eric Berry.

Even in the dark I could tell the group was a little down, and I'm not sure they really wanted to see two giddy Auburn fans, but they let us in because they are nice people. Had the tables been turned, I would have kissed them good-bye faster than Joshua Harris.

We watched two episodes of *MythBusters* while waiting for traffic to clear. The hosts were launching some sort of missile at a compact car, then showing the impact in incredibly slow slow motion—perhaps there is a myth that missiles are unable to destroy cheap cars.[7] The first ten times I saw it were cool, but after that I got bored and began talking to the darkened silhouette next to me.

"So you're the guy writing the book about faith and football?"

"Yep," I said. "I'm going to a game at every school in the SEC this season."

"Wait," he said. "How can you visit every school in one season?"

"Well, there are thirteen weeks, so I just had to make a schedule and go."

"Yeah, but there are sixteen teams in the SEC."

This is when I realized I was probably talking to some library rat who'd never stepped foot in Neyland Stadium. "No," I told him. "There are only twelve teams in the SEC."

"Oh," he said, not really believing me.

We watched as another myth was busted by dropping mannequins off the Hoover Dam, then one of the guys said the VFC house was now closing. Someone flipped on the light, and I looked over to say good-bye to my friend who thought Joe Paterno was the bad guy from the *Home Alone* movies, only to see he was decked out head-to-toe in UT orange and had taken the time to painstakingly paint his face like Tennessee's checkerboard end zone.

---

7. Busted.

Welcome to the SEC, where even people who know nothing about football are fanatical about it.

• • •

The next morning Tricia and I attended a worship service at Park West Church of God in Knoxville. I was excited about this because for the first thirty-one years of my life I had never heard anyone speak in tongues. And while Park West's website didn't actually *say* there would be tongues, my denominational preconceptions told me tongues was *all* there'd be.[8] Park West meets in a gorgeous 1,000-seat sanctuary about five miles west of Neyland Stadium. There was a good crowd that morning, and I noticed boxes of tissues placed at the end of each pew. "See," I told Tricia, pointing at the tissues. "Weeping is a given. They'll be slaying people in the Spirit in no time." Tricia said the tissues were probably there because of H1N1, but I kept the faith.

Five singers, a ten-piece rock band, and a backup choir led corporate worship. The songs were upbeat, and soon the younger folks in the congregation were jumping with their hands in the air. About thirty-five minutes of this was followed by a time of prayer, where many went down to the altar, and most returned weeping. I gave Tricia a knowing smirk. Some men came down and took up the weekly offering, then a young pastor named Jeremy McGinnis took the pulpit. We'd already been at Park West for an hour.

Jeremy is the son of Park West's lead pastor, Gerald McGinnis. He was apparently back at Park West from a stint at another church, and everyone seemed happy he returned. So happy they didn't mind listening to him preach for an hour. Tricia and I, however, attend a Southern Baptist church in Birmingham that is tele-

---

8. When I was a kid, a friend told me at the Church of God people speak in tongues. Most likely he was referring to a specific Church of God; however, I attributed this new information to all Churches of God worldwide.

vised, meaning we know, almost to the minute, what time church will end every Sunday. Ten minutes into Dr. McGinnis's sermon, my stomach was speaking in tongues, and I was having a hard time listening to anything else. The only thing I even vaguely recall was that in the opening, Pastor Jeremy said he was driving in his truck the day before and he had to pull over because he couldn't stop crying. "And I wasn't crying because Tennessee had lost *another* football game," he added to the groans of the congregation.

Poor Tennessee: even their preachers had lost faith.

In the end we never heard anyone speak in tongues, which was disappointing, but nothing could keep me down too long. Auburn was 5–0, and instead of becoming more balanced, I was becoming insufferable. My idle thoughts would run wild with visions of a national championship, and what Gene Chizik lifting that crystal trophy would mean to me. A part of me even thought if Auburn were to win it all, perhaps then I could go on with my life, maybe do some great things. The more I thought about it, the more it made sense. God would give us the title while I wrote this book; then with my newfound fame I could travel the globe preaching my message of a healthy perspective toward sports. But Auburn had to win it all first. Because what if I were off doing great things when it happened? I'd never forgive myself.

But a funny thing happened on the way to our national title. Well, *funny* might not be the right word, unless you think getting blown out by Arkansas is hilarious. And Tennessee, well they were only seven days away from trouncing the Georgia Bulldogs. In fact, the next time I called my Vols friends, they were more than happy to tell me all about the Big Orange. Faith, it seems, is a fickle thing.

LOUISIANA STATE UNIVERSITY

OCTOBER 10, 2009

Dance in the kitchen 'till the morning light: Louisiana Saturday night!

Bob McDill, "Louisiana Saturday Night"

"HEY, BOY, how much you askin' for your wife?"

Those were the last words I recall hearing as we made our hasty exit from LSU's Tiger Stadium late in the third quarter of the 2003 Auburn–LSU game. The Bayou Bengals had just taken a 24–7 lead, and the surrounding hoard of opposing fans, who up until that point had only been mildly abusive, became increasingly hostile. Tricia and I gave a quick nod to our friends Lori and Jeremy, and without saying a word the four of us began the long walk down the bleachers, a walk made longer still by a serenade of taunts from the LSU faithful. Then, just as we neared the safety of an exit tunnel, a man who appeared to have come to the game straight from the pages of a Stephen King novel grabbed Jeremy by the shoulder and made the generous offer to take Lori off his hands. (For future reference, when someone asks how much money you'd take for your wife, the correct reply is not, "She's just my girlfriend.")

When the lights of Baton Rouge finally disappeared from our rearview mirror, Tricia and I vowed to never again return to Tiger Stadium. We felt fortunate to be alive, and that we'd been given a second chance in life like George Bailey at the end of *It's a Wonderful Life*. Once home I had to fight the urge to run through town wishing a Merry Christmas to the wonderful old Building and Loan.

For five years I kept my promise of never returning to what I considered the Beirut of South Central Louisiana, but then I had this harebrained notion to tour the SEC, and despite my best efforts to have LSU moved to the Big 12 for the season, I had to go back. So I resigned myself to the distinct possibility of being fed to alligators by a group of LSU fans who warned me they'd do just that if I ever again set foot in their stadium. But then it hit me: I didn't have to go back to an *Auburn* game — I could go anytime I wanted to! I could even wear purple and gold. In fact, if I got to be one of them for a few hours, it might actually be fun, especially if I were there for, say, #1 Florida vs. #4 LSU.

Some friends had their doubts. Not that I would have fun in Tiger Stadium posing as an LSU fan — everyone thought that sounded fun in the same sort of way that running with the bulls sounds fun. But many had shared a similar experience to mine on their trips to LSU, and they voiced the opinion that I would have trouble finding a single Christian in town to talk to. Baton Rouge, as far as they were concerned, was Gomorrah with a Top 5 football team.

Yet soon my inbox was flooded with messages from all sorts of Christ-following Tiger fans. What I didn't realize at the time was that half of those emails were from Vick Green.

Vick's first email came at 3:51 p.m. on July 18. It was written in a fast-paced stream of consciousness that would have confused William Faulkner. *"I am obsessed with LSU and have been since I could walk and know crazy facts like how many LSU players from the 1940s had fathers named Darryl."* I tried to decipher his email three or four times but gave up and started looking online to see if Babel Fish translated nonsense to English. Thankfully Vick sent another, more coherent, email at 4:37 p.m., and I was able to delete the first one, though I briefly considered publishing it as a lost poem of ee cummings.

Vick went on to explain, with much-appreciated clarity, that LSU football had been an idol in his life since long before he could walk. Growing up, he never missed a game, and like so many of us, his happiness was based solely on his team's successes and failures. But the Lord had been at work in Vick's life, slowly filling the void a false god like football inevitably leaves. Now Vick is a student at LSU and leads a Bible study for some thirty LSU football players. "It was a dream come true," he told me. "I've been given the opportunity to spread the gospel and keep guys like Drake Nevis and Russell Shepard accountable in their walk with Christ. Those guys have helped me understand what it's like to play for LSU, and that the game isn't everything. It seems once I put down my idol of LSU football, God blessed me with all I've ever asked for and more."

By the time I finished reading, I'd already decided to spend time with Vick during my trip to Baton Rouge. He seemed like the real deal—and besides, I wanted to meet Drake Nevis and Russell Shepard, in hopes of convincing them to transfer to Auburn.

A few weeks later, I spoke with Vick on the phone, and he

invited me to stay at his house while I was in Baton Rouge. I said yes but immediately regretted it because, in my haste to save money on a hotel room, I overlooked the fact I'm utterly terrified of LSU fans. In a matter of weeks I'd gone from saying I'd never visit Baton Rouge again to having a sleepover at the home of some crazy LSU student. That afternoon I went for a tetanus booster.

• • •

On most days the drive from Birmingham to Baton Rouge isn't what you'd call exhilarating, but that afternoon the occasional funnel cloud helped keep things interesting. I drove on edge, occasionally pulling over to let a blinding rain pass. Then, somewhere near Slidell, a couple of eighteen-wheelers got in a fight and turned I–10 into a parking lot. I was already running late, so I sent Vick a text message to let him know when to expect me.

> Me: Running late. Car wreck.
> Vick: U were in a wreck? R U OK?
> Me: NO! Other cars. I'm stuck in traffic.
> Vick: LOL OK B safe. I've got a surprise guest when U get here.
> Me: The Golden Girls?[1] You know I'm married right?
> Vick: No.
> Me: Gerry DiNardo? Shaquille O'Neal? James Carville?
> Vick: No, No, No. U can meet him when U get here.
> Me: Mike the Tiger, Fats Domino, Huey P. Long?
> Vick: Just B safe.

The suspense made sitting in traffic even worse, but eventually the road was cleared, and I made my triumphant, if cautious,

---

1. I was talking about the leggy dance girls that accompany the LSU Marching Band, not the geriatrics from that eighties sitcom, you weirdos.

return to Baton Rouge. Vick lived in a nice neighborhood a few miles from campus. Kegs and children's toys littered the front yards, the comical result of a developer's dream to have families and college kids share a housing development. Vick was waiting outside when I arrived, and he greeted me with a man hug. He took my bags, and I followed him inside, where at least twenty-five guys were playing NCAA 2010 on four Xbox 360s. "We've got a tournament drawn up," Vick said. "We gave you Auburn, and you're playing next."

My eyes lit up. I don't like to throw around words like *prodigy* and *wunderkind*, but in my parents' den I was certainly the Bobby Fisher of video game football. Since 1993 I had been dominating my friends, and I am quite certain I invented the spread offense fifteen years ago by mistake. I glanced around the room and relished the thought of sending each and every one of those kids home in painful humiliation.

Turns out it was Vick's birthday, and to celebrate he was having friends over for ping-pong and video games. There were no girls at the house, but that is usually the case wherever there is a video game tournament. Vick shouted introductions across the room, then took me into the kitchen, where a guy was bringing in some burgers from an outside grill. "Here's your surprise," Vick said. I took a good look at the guy but didn't recognize him, then wondered if perhaps he was a famous character actor like Burgess Meredith. "So nice to meet you," I said, extending my hand and hoping his voice would clue me in on what movies he'd been in.

"Hey," he said. "I'm Greg Marsh."

Greg Marsh, Greg Marsh, where do I know Greg Marsh?

"He's a Bama fan," Vick said with a laugh. "I didn't say he was a *good* surprise."

My first game in the nearly thirty-man video game tournament was against Vick's friend Holden Scyster, who had chosen to play with the USC Trojans. The folks at EA Sports apparently think a lot of USC. Either that or Holden had entered a cheat code[2] that gave his players the powers of the Watchmen. Another problem was the Xbox 360 controller, which had seven or eight more buttons than I remember video game controllers having. Holden was up 21–0 after about three minutes and the mercy rule was mercifully invoked. My once prodigious talent had faded in old age—but I am married to a real-life female, which is more than Holden Scyster can say.

The night and the tournament wore on, and during one of the semifinals, Vick's roommate Nathan Marceaux performed a shirtless celebration dance, only to have his touchdown reversed by an instant replay review. *When did video games get instant replay?* And as much as I wanted to stay up and see who took home the title of "Least Likely to Kiss a Girl Anytime Soon," I asked Vick to show me an extra bed where I could sleep.

The bed actually belonged to Vick's other roommate, Max Adams, a biochemistry major with a slight obsession with ants. I had to move stacks of books about ants off the bed just to make room to lie down. Then I noticed the walls were covered with posters of ants, and the shelves were full of ant models and ants in jars and ants running farms. My head is starting to itch again just thinking about it. Needless to say, I did not sleep well—especially when the twenty-five LSU guys started a fight with the one Bama fan over which animal, an elephant or tiger, would win in a fight to the death.

Did I mention there weren't any girls at Vick's party?

● ● ●

The next morning I drove to the home of Father Gerald Burns, pastor of St. Aloysius Catholic Church in Baton Rouge. Father Burns

---

2. Up, up, down, down, left, right, left, right, b, a, select, start.

had graciously volunteered to spend some time with me and discuss his passion for the Bayou Bengals. I arrived that morning expecting ... well, I don't know what I was expecting, really, but certainly not a sixty-six-year-old priest who was built like a linebacker and owned a fifty-five-inch HDTV for watching football games.

We sat down, and Father Burns began to tell stories. He grew up selling programs at Tiger Stadium in the early 1950s. Back then, he told me, Catholic seminaries would recruit young men for the priesthood, and he left home in his early teens. "At school only the juniors and seniors were allowed to stay up on Saturday nights to listen to LSU games. So we underclassmen would wake up Sunday mornings just dying to talk to the older kids to find out how the Tigers fared the night before. I didn't hear about Billy Cannon's Halloween Run until the following Sunday morning, and that was from the kid next to me at the urinal. I asked what happened and he almost wet himself trying to get it all out, 'OleMisswasleadingthreetonothingallgame, butBillyCannontookapunt, andhebrokeseventackles, thenheraneightyyardsforthescore, andwewonseventothree!'"

During his years at the seminary, Father Burns saw only one LSU game in person. A family member was getting married, and he was allowed to spend one night away from school. He wisely chose Saturday night, and after the wedding he saw his Tigers dismantle the Florida Gators. I asked if he thought history could repeat itself later that evening, and he said, "It'll be very tough. I think LSU is probably a year away."

He told me about all the games he'd seen. The Earthquake Game against Auburn was a particular favorite, and he relished retelling the game's final minute and the seismic celebration that almost broke Louisiana loose from the rest of the continent.[3] But his best story by far was the 1970 LSU–Ole Miss game.

---

3. Let's hope Thomas Jefferson bought the extended warranty.

It was Archie Manning's senior season, and the future sire of Super Bowl–winning quarterbacks entered the game with a broken arm. Despite the fact teams in those days could keep hundreds of players on scholarship, Ole Miss apparently did not have anyone else to play quarterback, so they sent Archie out to face the LSU defense with his arm in a cast. It did not go well. In fact, LSU won 61–17.

"It was a pretty wild scene," Father Burns said, "as I'm sure you can imagine. The crowd started chanting, 'Go to hell, Ole Miss, go to hell!' and I got a little carried away and joined in. The woman sitting in front of me, an Ole Miss fan, whirled around and saw me up there in my priestly garb telling her team where to go. She called me a bad sport and threatened to report me to my superiors. So I asked her if she knew how many seats were in Tiger Stadium. She said she did not, so I informed her there were in fact 67,620 seats, and if she didn't like the one she was in, she was more than welcome to find a new one."

I just hung my head and laughed, then asked Father Burns if he regretted the incident. He smiled and said, "I regret I wore my collar to the game."

Of course that's just another way of saying I wish people didn't know who I am, and we all wish that from time to time. Like when you refuse to let a car with a rival team's license plate merge into traffic, then later wish you didn't have a Jesus fish on your car. If you go to a game these days, it is a guarantee that someone in close proximity to you will embarrass themselves by dropping F-bombs in front of their small children or berating a player to the point that everyone around is uncomfortable. I don't have much of a temper, thank God, but the running commentary in my head is no better than the garbage spewing from the mouths of others. In times like that, I'm embarrassed God knows who I am.

●　●　●

I drove back to Vick's house and watched the first half of the Auburn–Arkansas game, which was about as fun as watching someone kick your dog for two hours. Vick said some folks from his college ministry were having a tailgate, and I said we should go, if not for any other reason than in hopes that a change of my venue might alter Auburn's luck. Before we left, Vick gave me a gold LSU T-shirt to wear. It was too tight, and I looked absurd, but at least now I felt safe.

The tailgate wasn't so much a tailgate as a pool party without swimming. We were in the backyard of a house near campus with a pool, though the water was too cold for even the LSU crazies to jump in. A couple of guys had built a contraption that let them cook an entire pig inside a wooden box. The pig had apparently been cooking for close to a day and was supposed to be ready at any moment.

I sat down to watch the Auburn game, and things were actually looking up. My Tigers had somehow managed to score twenty-one points in five minutes, cutting the deficit to a manageable margin. Every so often an LSU fan would walk up, say something disparaging about Auburn, then walk away. I like to think that had they known I was an Auburn grad, they would have held their tongues. Of course, minutes later Arkansas was once again leading by three touchdowns, and I, too, was saying disparaging things about Auburn.

Someone yelled that the pig was finally ready to eat, and we all stood around the box to see what it would look like once the lid was raised. It still looked like a pig. Two guys with knives that could have been mistaken for swords started hacking it up, and soon plates were being passed around and we were told to dig in. The problem was, for me at least, the pig's head was still sitting on the table, smiling. It was just a little too much like *Lord of the Flies*. I knew soon someone would be blowing in a conch shell, telling us to kill a fat kid with glasses, and I didn't want to be a part of it. So I asked Vick to show me around campus.

LSU's campus was exactly how I remembered it. The buildings look foreign almost, like I'd taken a wrong turn near Ponchatoula and wound up in the Italian Renaissance. But once I heard the chants of "Tiger bait! Tiger bait!" I knew exactly where I was.

The tailgating scene in Baton Rouge is both tasty and menacing. LSU fans always seem to be in an aggressive posture, just waiting for an opposing fan to stroll by so they can verbally pummel them. But if those opposing fans just had the nerve to stop and say hello, they would be offered a seat at the table of Cajun deliciousness.

Last summer I asked Deacon Richard Grant, associate pastor at Our Lady of Mercy Church, if he thought fasting could change the outcome of games. "I hope not," he said. "If so, LSU would not be a very good team. Our tailgating food is way too good to fast from." And he is right.

The tailgates have entertainment too, and not just cornhole. Music is more prevalent in Baton Rouge than any other stop in the SEC. All the tailgates have something playing, and some even have live bands, but only at LSU do you see people dancing alone to music only they can hear.

Vick and I met up with his friend Holden, the guy who used a cheat code to beat me at video game football, and the three of us went to LSU's Tiger Walk. We waited for the team behind barricades, and across the way young children held signs that were both hilarious and appalling.

One read, "Where is Tim Tebow when you need him ... unconscious." This was a reference to the famous concussion the Florida quarterback had suffered two weeks earlier against Kentucky. Tebow's blackout had been national news and even had Congress debating whether helmets should be made safer.

Another sign read, "For God so loved the world that he gave us Chad Jones." I pointed it out to Vick, and he said, "Don't look at me. I didn't write it."

The team marched down the hill in front of us to fervent cheers from the LSU masses. A few minutes later the band arrived, marching into place at the top of the hill, then pausing just a moment for dramatic effect. Bum, Buh, Bum, Bum! The first notes of "Tiger Rag" rang out into the cool fall night, and every LSU fan in earshot started foaming at the mouth. The band began to hop in place, then ran in formation down the hill to the chants of LSU! LSU! LSU!

When this party ended, I joined the bigger party inside Tiger Stadium. Max, Vick's ant-loving roommate, had given me his ticket to the game, which meant I would be sitting in what is, without a doubt, the wildest student section in America. But if I was going to get into the game, first I'd have to get through the gate, where stern-looking men were checking student IDs in hopes of busting any thirty-one-year-old Christian humorist who tried to sneak in. The dark-haired girl behind me looked worried. She showed me her ID, which belonged to a blonde girl that was obviously not her. "Just tell them you let your roots grow out," I offered. She smiled weakly. "You've got a better shot than I do," I said. "I graduated college in 2002."

"Yeah," she said. "You're not getting in. I thought you were someone's dad."

But I did get in. The kid in front of us got pulled from the line because his ID was invalid, and while he pitched a fit, we were all able to slip through with little notice. My brunette friend gave me a quick high five, and then I found Vick and Holden and our seats.

Being in that stadium for the first time in five years brought back a flood of memories, all of them terrifying. I kept thinking the students would look past my T-shirt and into my soul, discovering that I wasn't an LSU student or even a fan. Of course my inability to do any of the cheers might have tipped them off as well.

LSU fans have cheers and dances for every occasion. If the Tigers record a safety, the band plays "Hey Jude" and everyone belly dances. If LSU has a first down called back for offensive pass interference, fans turn to the east and raise both fists while the trumpet section plays "Taps." I should have been studying this stuff since summer, and now Vick was trying to teach me in the five minutes prior to kickoff. It wasn't going to happen.

The game opened with LSU driving the ball to midfield before stalling out and being forced to punt. A great punt pinned Florida down around the five-yard line, and the recently concussed Tim Tebow led the Gators onto the field right in front of the LSU student section.

I don't recall ever hearing sound the way I heard it at that moment. It sat on my chest like the fat bully from gym class. I wondered how the Florida players would even hear the snap count. They couldn't. False start, half the distance to the goal line, and Tiger Stadium went *Spinal Tap* and turned the noise up to eleven.

But then Florida tight end Aaron Hernandez did something I wasn't expecting. He turned to the LSU student section and raised his hands as if to say, "That's all you've got? I thought you guys were supposed to be loud." I realized then the defending national champion Gators weren't nearly as intimidated as I was.

Florida proceeded to drive the ball across midfield and kick a field goal, which LSU would later match. Then Tebow got hot, and the Gators went eighty yards in eight plays to take a 10–3 lead into halftime.

It was one of those close games that never felt close. Vick told me he was pleasantly surprised the deficit was no more than seven points, and I kept thinking the same thing.

The third quarter accomplished nothing, as neither team was able to score. Then about midway through the fourth quarter, the Gators added another field goal to take a 13–3 lead, which was pretty much insurmountable. The crowd was deflated, and the party-like atmosphere from a few hours back now felt like a funeral. And not one of those fun New Orleans funerals with bands and clowns, either. This was a sad normal-person funeral.

After the game, Vick and I waited outside the players' entrance to talk to Drake Nevis, who despite the loss had played an incredible game. One by one the players walked out, looking sullen, only to light up at the sight of their families and friends. Drake finally left the locker room, only to be greeted by Vick and me, but he smiled all the same and gave Vick a big hug. They talked for a minute about what church service to attend the next morning, then we let Drake go home for some much-needed rest.

Seeing the players like this was weird, surrounded by loved ones who could not have been prouder, even though Florida had won the game. It was weird because I knew out on the interstate people were sitting in traffic, cursing these same kids because they lost by ten points to the number one team in the nation. But the players and their families seem to have figured something out, something they have passed on to Vick: football is only a game. You remember games, right? You remember playing football in the backyard with the kids from the neighborhood? Well, really, this is no different. Except back then grown men and women didn't attach their happiness to the outcome of your backyard scrum. It was good for me to see this, and I hope the next time I feel personally slighted because an Auburn player drops a pass or misses a field goal I'll think of this scene and remind myself to stop being an idiot.

• • •

The next morning I attended my first Catholic mass at St. Aloysius Catholic Church and felt almost as out of place as I did the night before in the student section. Catholics, like LSU fans, seem to incorporate a lot of hand motions that I, despite owning the *Godfather* DVD, just don't know. I would try to keep up, but I was always a few steps behind and would sometimes revert back to the cheers I'd learned the night before. Like when I bowed repeatedly at Father Burns as if he'd just forced the Gators to punt.

Father Burns talked about the game a little during his sermon, even calling it a tragic weekend with a wry smile, but he also told us that he'd given away his ticket to the game. "I just can't do those late-night games anymore and still be the best priest I can be," he said. "Because this, this here, this is what's really important to me."

When I heard Father Burns say this, I thought of Victor Thompson, the Tennessee music minister who would occasionally lead worship after a night without sleep. I fought the urge to rank him against Father Burns, then decide where I fit between them on the Christian-fan scale, because that is no way to go through this life. Father Burns decided what was most important, and then decided attending a late-night football game was a hindrance. Mr. Thompson did the same thing and decided seeing friends and family in Knoxville was worth the effort. If my relationship with God truly is what's most important to me, then that is what I should focus on, not how many football games I can go to before I think God is mad at me. Because the question isn't how much football is okay with God, and the quicker I realize that, the better.

● ● ●

Driving home, I made a quick detour through the LSU campus, stopping at the home of Mike the Tiger, LSU's 300-pound Siberian-Bengal tiger mascot. Families were there with children, taking pictures and trying to get the disinterested tiger to look in their direction. I started thinking about LSU fans and how my opinion of them had changed over the weekend. Like tigers, they should probably be kept in cages. Wait, that's not what I mean. I mean that, like tigers, LSU fans are cute when they're young but will eat you when they're older. No, that's not it either. I think what I'm trying to say is that LSU fans are people, just like you and me, who love their God and love their team and really love Saturday nights in the fall. So if you ever get the chance to go down there and watch a football game, you'd better go. And you'd better call me, because I can't wait to go back.

WEEK 6

UNIVERSITY OF FLORIDA

OCTOBER 17, 2009

Superman wears Tim Tebow pajamas.

The Internet

YOU COULD TELL REVEREND J. W. ARNOLD was not happy. His sermon had come to a complete halt, and now he was just staring at us through a set of eyes that would give a marine pause. His breathing grew heavier, and his hair, which had been neatly combed to one side, was now reaching toward the heavens, making him look like an irate Cosmo Kramer. We all waited, diverting our eyes from the man who would soon be scolding us for our unknown sin. Then it came.

"If you don't want to be here this morning," he shouted, "go listen to Tebow!"

I had no clue what Rev. Arnold was so upset about. He seemed to think we, and by *we* I mean Tricia and me and all of the Pentecostals of Gainesville, were not being a very responsive congregation. But in my life I have never seen a church respond more to what a preacher was saying than that morning. Whenever Rev.

Arnold would raise his voice, men and women would leap from their pews and shout amens until they were told to take a seat. Of course, I don't know what a typical Sunday morning is like for the Pentecostals of Gainesville, so maybe they were phoning it in.

Rev. Arnold was correct that listening to Tebow was a viable option. Not *Tim* Tebow, mind you, but his father, *Bob* Tebow, who was speaking this particular Sunday morning at North Central Baptist Church, less than a football field away from the Pentecostals' parking lot. This was the reason cars were parked up and down Northwest Twenty-third Avenue, and perhaps the reason Rev. Arnold, who doesn't care much for the Gators, was more than a little agitated.

● ● ●

Tricia and I had arrived in Gainesville two nights earlier. It was homecoming week at the University of Florida, which meant parades and pep rallies and all other sorts of festive happenings, including Gator Growl. Now in its eighty-sixth year, Gator Growl is part pep rally, part variety show. On the docket this night were, and I'm not making this up, O.A.R., Dana Carvey, and Jabba-WockeeZ (those white-faced dancing guys from the Gatorade G commercials). Unfortunately, or perhaps fortunately, we arrived in Gainesville just as Gator Growl 2009 was coming to an end.

However, we *were* in time for the Later Growl, a post pep rally extravaganza at the University of Florida's Baptist Campus Ministry (BCM) with food, music, and—for those who like to mix their fellowship with extreme sports—a climbing wall.

We were greeted by Eddie Gilley, director of the BCM, and David Wood and his wife, Tami, who serve as assistant directors. I had been in contact with them for a few months, so it was nice to put faces with their names, though it was even nicer to put their free food in my mouth.

David introduced us to Kaleb Erwin, an aerospace engineering major and student president of the BCM. Tricia and I asked Kaleb the kinds of questions you typically ask college students. What's your major? What do you plan to do after graduation? What is the air speed velocity of an unladen swallow? And Kaleb kindly answered all our queries with a smile that just got under my skin.

"I'm going to be honest with you," I told Kaleb. "I'm a little sick of watching you guys live this charmed life. First you win the basketball title, and you're not even a freaking basketball school. Then you get Tebow, and you win the BCS title in the same stupid year! Then, somehow, you convince that entire basketball team to stay and play another season, even though one of them needs the NBA money because his family is living in a box somewhere, and they win another title." At this point I'm pulling my own hair and Tricia is slowly backing away so people won't think we're together. "Then Tebow wins the Heisman as a sophomore, which is such a fairy tale even Disney wouldn't believe it. And now you've won another BCS title, you're ranked number one in the nation, and we, the rest of the world, we're just a little sick of it all."

Kaleb just smiled at me, so I continued.

"Just tell me what it's like! What does it feel like to wake up each morning a Florida fan? Is it like Snow White? Do birds pull back your sheets while chipmunks dress you in the latest national championship gear? Do alligators place orange and blue Crocs on your feet so you can walk outside to get today's edition of the *Gainesville Sun*, which probably had to devote a special section to all the five-star recruits your team just signed? Geez!"

Again, Kaleb just smiled.

Tricia tried to take over and ask Kaleb the types of questions I'd normally ask were I not temporarily insane with jealousy, like, Has your love of football ever caused you to get upset and say or do something you'd later regret?

"No," Kaleb said. "Not that I can think of."

"Of course, it hasn't," I butted in. "It's not like his team ever loses or breaks his heart. What's he have to get upset about? 'Crap, my team only won by thirty-eight points, guess I'd better go register FireUrbanMeyer.com.' Every day of his life is perfect!"

About that time I got a call from Cody Davidson, another Florida senior who was just leaving the Gator Growl and was coming by to say hello. Cody is a big, athletic kid with a Grizzly Adams beard. He also plays rugby for Florida, and the thought of him slamming me to the ground made me hesitant to berate him for attending a school with successful athletic programs. So when he arrived, I toned it down a bit.

We talked about football as a hindrance to faith, and Cody admitted, "Saturdays in the fall are terrible for my quiet time. Either the game is early and I have to rush to the Swamp, or it's a late game and the day is full of tailgating and whatnot. It's a shame, but God, Jesus, and the Bible rarely cross my mind on football Saturdays."

Cody went on to tell us in great detail just how superstitious he is concerning the Gators. "I have to wear the same hat, shirt, and shorts every week." He said he didn't go as far as underwear, but I don't believe him. "And I absolutely hate when we jingle our car keys at a team we are beating."

"Yeah, that's sort of classless," I said.

"No, it's not that," Cody said. "It's just bad luck. Every time we do it, teams start coming back on us. We nearly lost to Vanderbilt because of that stupid key thing!"

I liked Cody. He reminded me a lot of myself, were I tall and athletic with the ability to grow a beard. "Have you ever done anything at a game you would later regret?"

A big smile flashed across his face, and he told us, "Last week at the LSU game, this six-year-old kid beside me wouldn't stop chanting 'Tiger bait! Tiger bait!' so I grabbed him by the shoulders and told him Santa Claus wasn't real."

"Wow," Tricia said. "What did the kid do?"

"He just started chanting 'Tiger bait! Tiger bait!' louder."

"Yeah, that sounds about right."

I've been to Baton Rouge as a visitor, so I could totally understand screaming at a child. What really got me thinking was when Cody talked about superstitions. Tricia and I play the same CD every game, in 2004 I wore the same shirt every week, and if I'm at home watching the game, I constantly change seats because I fear the one I'm in is causing Auburn to play poorly. I think what it really boils down to is I want to feel like I am part of the team. I want to believe something I do or say can have an effect on the game's outcome. Were I wealthy, I'd probably donate barrels of money to the athletic department so they'd plaster my name on the stadium, but even so, I'd still just be a fan, and nothing more.

It was now close to midnight, and the Later Growl was set to rage on until at least 2:00 a.m., but only food poisoning can keep me up that late, so we drove back to our hotel in Alachua for a good night's sleep.

The next morning we woke up early and drove back to Gainesville. As we walked around, I remembered how much I love the look of Florida's campus, especially the historic district, which consists of nineteen buildings and dormitories centered around the Century Tower, a 157-foot carillon tower whose bells chime out Jimmy Buffett songs every day at noon. Admittedly I flunked out of architecture after only one quarter, but I admire the design of the buildings. The style is what I would call "Florida-y." That may not be an actual architectural term, but I don't know the real word for "brick buildings surrounded by palm trees."

All the walking made us hungry, and the allure of free hamburgers took us back to the BCM. Folks were sitting inside watching the Oklahoma–Texas game on a massive projector in the BCM's main hall. Tricia and I fixed our burgers and sat down next to Kaleb Erwin who, like half the people in the room, was wearing a Tim Tebow jersey. Kaleb introduced us to Zach Allen, college minister at North Central Baptist Church, who was not and never would be wearing a Tebow jersey.

"I'm a Florida State grad," Zach told us.

"How'd you end up here?" I asked.

"Near the end of seminary I began praying for an opportunity to work with college students," Zach said. Then he added with a smile, "I guess I learned my lesson about praying more specifically."

We ate our burgers and watched Oklahoma quarterback Sam Bradford's college career end when he reinjured his shoulder on the second drive of the game. Bradford had edged out Tebow for the 2008 Heisman Trophy, and our conversation inevitably turned to the man whose #15 jersey had become Gainesville's latest fashion trend.[1] With Tim Tebow's unmatched success and his willingness to preach the gospel anytime a microphone is near, I wondered if perhaps there had been a spiritual awakening on the Florida campus.

"I wouldn't say there has been a spiritual awakening," Kaleb told me. "Tebow isn't some one-man revival, baptizing people in his accounting class."

"No," Zach agreed. "This is still a very secular public university. But when Tim speaks on campus at FCA or Crusade, the crowds are unbelievable. Of course that can be a problem, too."

"How so?" I asked.

"He can't really go to church in Gainesville anymore. Not without getting mobbed before and after the service. Coach Meyer has

---

1. You thought I was about to make a joke about jean shorts didn't you? Well, I'm better than that.

a 4:00 p.m. Sunday worship just for the team so they can worship in peace."

Kaleb told me he'd heard it was worse in Jacksonville at Tebow's home church, where after a service the star quarterback is likely to spend an hour autographing children's Bibles.

"Kids ask him to sign their Bibles?" I asked, more shocked parents would let their kids do this than anything else. I mean, I once asked Kareem Abdul-Jabbar to autograph a Koran, but come on.

I suppose Tim Tebow doesn't have to stay around and meet these children. He could rush out a side door or even have the pastor announce that he is there to worship not meet fans. But perhaps Tim thinks this is part of his ministry, talking to young people and giving them a great example to follow. Nevertheless, asking someone to autograph a book he didn't write is kind of odd.

We finally left the BCM and walked west down University Avenue, passing the Catholic Gator tailgate, where I snapped a picture of their sign, which read, "Champions Pray," then immediately emailed it to Auburn coach Gene Chizik. It was a beautiful day, and we were enjoying ourselves until I began to panic because we still didn't have tickets to the game.

Florida was hosting the Arkansas Razorbacks, and despite the fact it was homecoming, I didn't foresee us having much trouble finding tickets. Then again, I didn't foresee Tricia giving me a $120 spending limit, so I was starting to get a little worried.

Scalpers are apparently not allowed to scalp on campus, so they congregate across University Avenue, asking everyone who walks past them, "How many you got? How many you need?"

The answers to these questions were none and two, though Tricia insisted if I could only find one ticket for a reasonable price then she'd be fine watching the game from a sports bar. But after walking by an establishment called Balls, where two scantily clad women were hanging out a window offering drinks to everyone who passed, I decided we were either both going to the game or we were both going home.

I generally detest dealing with scalpers—not because I dislike them as people, but because I am uncomfortable with the bargaining system as a whole. My standard approach is to loiter near one, in hopes someone will inquire about the dozens of tickets he is currently holding in his hand. The scalper will then quote a price I find affordable, at which point I jump in with cash in hand to purchase the tickets out from under the initial inquirer. This has never actually happened.

Scalpers never give you their rock-bottom price. They prefer a back and forth, a give and take, a dance if you will. I hate dancing. I want scalpers to be more like CarMax: no haggle.

"How much?"

"How much are you looking to spend?"

This is a stupid question, because I don't want to spend any, but I think scalpers are bound by law to ask it. Tricia had given me a limit of $60 per ticket, so I thought I'd at least indulge this guy and said I was looking to spend $100.

"One hundred dollars a ticket," he said. "I think I might be able to work with you."

"No, not $100 a ticket. I want two tickets for $100."

He just started laughing and told his scalper friend, "This guy wants two tickets for $100." They all laughed at us, then one of them said, "You two must not really want to go to the game."

"No," I said. "Not particularly."

This confused them, so they reverted back to their mantra of, "How many you got? How many you need?"

I suggested we walk across the street to campus and try to look pitiful in hopes some benevolent alumnus would shower compassion on our struggle for affordable admission. Tricia didn't have any better ideas, so we started walking around the entrance to Ben

Hill Griffin Stadium, joining hundreds of others who were holding two fingers in the air.

It didn't look good, but within minutes a couple of kids were tugging at my shirt. At first I thought they wanted me to sign their Bible, but they pointed us toward two older men who were smiling and waving in our direction. We walked over, and one of the men said, "We've got two extra for $100."

"Yes," I moaned. "A hundred each."

"No." He laughed. "One hundred for the two. We just want to get rid of them."

I couldn't pay the man fast enough. We took our tickets and went to find our seats, though Tricia wanted to walk back to the scalper's corner and taunt the hagglers with our face-value tickets.

The Swamp, as Florida's stadium is affectionately known, is perhaps the most recognizable stadium in all of college football. That familiar orange façade and the four corners painted with twenty-foot letters ("This is ... GATOR COUNTRY") mean you can only be one place.

Our seats turned out to be on the forty-seven-yard line, about twenty rows up — quite possibly the best seats I've ever had for a sporting event, even ones I was playing in. The pregame atmosphere in Gainesville was sleepy, but day games can be that way, especially coming off a Top 5 matchup the previous week. But when Albert, the Gator mascot, took the field to lead the crowd in "Two Bits," things got a little rowdy.

You know the cheer. *Two bits, four bits, six bits, a dollar. All for the Gators, stand up and holler.* At Auburn the students audibly groan when this cheer is called for, but Florida fans love it, thanks to George Edmondson Jr., aka Mr. Two Bits, who led the cheer from 1949 to 2008. Now a six-foot alligator leads the cheer while wearing a yellow oxford shirt with an orange and blue tie. It's a bizarre scene, but one of my favorite traditions.

The game began, and the first quarter passed without scoring but not without incident. Our glorious seats were on the aisle, and I vaguely recall Tricia saying, "He doesn't look so good," as a fantastically drunk kid stumbled down to the seats below. Now, midway through the opening quarter, he was stumbling back up the bleachers and looking a little green in the face. A girl, perhaps an embarrassed girlfriend, was helping him walk, and the two of them crashed into a man standing in the aisle just to my left. Moments later, everyone in a ten-foot diameter was in the vomit splash zone, including yours truly.

I tried not to look at my arm and ran up to the bathroom to wash off what I knew was there. The kid and his girlfriend came in behind me, and she held his head over a garbage barrel while he finished what he started back on the twentieth row. "This isn't supposed to happen to people with fifty-yard-line seats," I yelled at him as I walked out. He briefly lifted his head, then stuck it back in the garbage.

The second quarter saw Arkansas take a 7–0 lead, and when the Florida offense continued to sputter, the home crowd grew a little restless. "Listen," Tricia said. Booing. Not a lot but enough that you could hear it. Tim Tebow and the Florida offense were jogging off the field to a smattering of boos. The two men next to us weren't booing, but they were ranting about how terrible the Florida offense had become. I wanted to scream, "Does no one here realize how fortunate they are?!"

Tim Tebow is everything you could ever want in a quarter-back—or a human being, for that matter. Growing up as an athlete, I used to tell God that if he would bless me with otherworldly athletic ability, then I would always thank him in press conferences, and I would wear Christian T-shirts under my uniform, and I would basically act just like Tim Tebow, though I'd never heard of Tebow at the time. God did not take me up on my offer, so now

I pray next time he makes someone like Tebow, will he please send him to Auburn.

Sure, most SEC fans have grown tired of the Tebow hype, but that isn't something Tim can control. He has always been gracious and humble and the kind of young man we would encourage our children to look up to. Not only that, I cannot imagine a fan in the country who wouldn't want Tim Tebow quarterbacking their team. And here he is, listening to a smattering of boos as he leaves the field. I looked at Tricia and said, "Florida fans don't deserve Tim Tebow."

"Well, who does deserve him?" she asked. "Certainly not us—we booed Brandon Cox two years ago."

Point taken. So I told her no one deserves him. "He should quit football right now."

Tricia just shook her head.

Arkansas took a 10–3 lead into the half, and I began to wonder if perhaps we were going to witness the number one team in America lose its homecoming game. I thought it might be a good story for the book, but it didn't look like losing would be an issue in the third quarter after Tebow hit Deonte Thompson on a seventy-seven-yard touchdown pass to give the Gators a 13–10 lead. The touchdown made Tebow the SEC's all-time leader in touchdowns with 123, but during the award ceremony Arkansas snuck down the field and kicked another field goal to tie the game at 13–13.

The third quarter came to a close, and at this point the entire stadium linked arms, began to sway, and sang "We Are the Boys from Old Florida," a peculiar song of debated origins. If you are ever fortunate enough to attend a game in the Swamp but are prone to seasickness, I suggest closing your eyes during this spectacle, because after watching 90,000 people sway back and forth for sixty seconds, I wanted to stick my head in the bathroom garbage can.

Arkansas struck first in the fourth quarter when Ryan Mallett hit Greg Childs for a seventy-five-yard touchdown pass. The men beside us left the game and never came back. They should have stayed, because in less than three minutes, Tebow had engineered another Gator scoring drive to tie the ball game 20–20. The Razorbacks took the kickoff and proceeded to march down the field, stopping at the Florida twenty-one-yard line to attempt a potential game-winning field goal. But Arkansas kicker Alex Tejada yanked the kick wide left, and Tim Tebow led the Gator offense onto the field with three minutes to play.

You know what happened next: Tebow completed three passes, rushed six times for twenty-two yards, and with nine seconds to play, Florida kicker Caleb Sturgis lined up a twenty-seven-yard field goal to win the game.

My friends around the SEC are always asking me which stadium is the loudest, hoping I will say theirs. The truth is I don't know. But I do know when Sturgis's kick split the uprights to give Florida a 23–20 win, I couldn't hear myself think, though I'm guessing my thoughts had just a hint of jealous rage.

● ● ●

After the kick, Tricia and I left the stadium in a sprint, hoping to find a sports bar showing the Auburn–Kentucky game. But we soon noticed we were in a footrace with hundreds of UF students who seemed intent on beating us to the bars. They are fast, and we are not, and by the time we got downtown, the bars were overflowing with jubilant Gator fans. So we walked sullenly down the street to have dinner at Firehouse Subs—and much to our surprise, they actually had the Auburn game on TV.

At halftime we left to visit Michael Kuhn, another UF senior and student president of RUF. Michael's apartment had what interior decorators would call a Gator motif. The walls were plastered with dozens of *Sports Illustrated* covers featuring great moments in Florida sports. Auburn, best I can figure, has been on the cover of *SI* four times. Florida was on the cover four times last month. Their success is appalling.

Michael's cable did not pick up the Auburn game, which was apparently on ESPN-Al Jazeera, so he pulled up the GameCast on his laptop, and we watched in horror as Kentucky's little blue line marched up and down the computer-generated field. Looking back, we could not have been ruder guests. I'd told Michael we wanted to come by so I could ask him a few questions for the book, but after Kentucky won 21 – 14, their first victory over Auburn since 1966, we said we were tired and went back to the hotel. The last thing I wanted to do was talk to another Florida fan about how hard it is to stay humble when you win everything.

I'm joking here a little, but they do have everything I want, and they got it all very quickly. Florida didn't win their first SEC championship until 1991, and now they have eight, to go along with three national championships. No wonder they got upset when the Gator offense sputtered early in the Arkansas game; they no longer have patience for sputtering. Which brings me back to an earlier thought that perhaps an Auburn national title would let me get on with my life. Now I'm not so sure. The winning starts to feel like a right, something you expect, something you are owed. No, Auburn winning a national title would not be the answer to my prayers, at least not the prayers I should be praying.

● ● ●

The next morning Tricia and I had breakfast with Brian Hinote, a recent UF graduate and lifetime member of the Pentecostals of Gainesville. "Rev. Arnold told us one Wednesday night about your book and said he had your contact information, but everyone was afraid to ask for it because we know how much he hates the Gators."

We followed Brian to church, and I'll admit I was a little apprehensive about meeting his Gator-hating pastor. But Rev. Arnold was very gracious, explaining to us he doesn't have a problem with people going to football games. "I don't think God does either," he said. "What bothers me, and what I think bothers God, is this spirit of idolatry associated with football in the South." We nodded, not wanting him to know we have two pictures of Bo Jackson in our house, and zero pictures of Jesus.

"I tell my people that I don't mind if they go to Gator games, but if they do, I want them to do three things. One, I want them to be as loud in this church as they are in the Swamp. Two, I want at least $50 from them, because I know that's the cheapest seat in the stadium. And three, if they can give the Gators four hours on Saturday, I want four hours on Sunday." Then he shook our hands and left us wondering if he meant we had to stay for four hours that morning.

The Pentecostals of Gainesville's service was incredible and incredibly loud. From now on when someone asks me what is the loudest stadium in the SEC, I will point them to this church. People were dancing on pews and running through the aisles. At one point Rev. Arnold yelled at us, "Gibbs family, I know you are Baptists, but it's okay to get a little excited this morning!"

The truth is I *was* excited, though the Baptist in me didn't really know how to show it. And if I'm honest with you, I was a touch envious. These folks were worshiping God the way I worship football players, and I was starting to realize how hollow my life becomes in the fall. I think I may have even been close to a spiritual epiphany, but then the man beside us started speaking in tongues and I sort of lost concentration.

● ● ●

While we drove home from Gainesville, I told Tricia I was still jealous. There's a part of me, a part I don't know how to shut up, that keeps thinking that if Auburn were to win a ton of basket-ball[2] and football titles, everything in my life would be perfect. Perhaps had I been a little older in 1992 I would have realized Alabama's championship really didn't alter my life in any way. But I was young, and so many years have passed that time has turned that football game into a jubilee where debts were canceled and we sang in the streets for days on end. And I tell myself a title for Auburn would be so different. We are the underdog; we are the little guy; we have one national championship, won twenty years before I was born. To add a second one all these years later, well, I'm not sure one fan base could handle that much joy. We truly might forgive our debtors and sing until the Second Coming.

But I was jealous of the Pentecostals as well. The passion I saw in that church beats anything I've seen in my life. And while I understand my denominational tendencies will probably never have me running around the sanctuary shouting to the Lord, I still would love to go through life as excited about God as they seem to be.

So it seems all I accomplished in Gainesville was finding things to be envious of. I saw football fans who have all they could ask for and more: national titles, Heisman Trophies, and enough *Sports Illustrated* covers to decorate an apartment. But I also saw Christians who were more excited to be with a fellowship of believers than they would've been to be in the Swamp. No matter what I do, I can't get the former. I can search from now till Judgment Day for a shirt so lucky that Auburn will win a title, but I'll never find it. It makes no difference how many times I change seats during a game, I have no effect on the outcome. There is nothing I can do to change Auburn football. As much as I think I am, I am not a part of it.

---

2. What? I can dream, can't I?

Here's the thing, and I think I understand it on a basic level: God wants to give me what the Pentecostals have. He wants to give me so much more than national titles and magazine covers. The energy and passion I saw, I could have that. God wants me to have it. But when God offers me those types of blessings, I say, "Thanks, but how about you keep that stuff and give Auburn a five-star quarterback instead?"

I know temporal things will let me down and leave me empty. Living in a culture of "buy this product; it will change your life," we all know this. But with football it seems to be a lesson I have to learn again each fall.

UNIVERSITY OF ALABAMA

OCTOBER 24, 2009

In Alabama, an atheist is someone who doesn't believe in Bear Bryant.

Wally Butts

"YOU KNOW ALABAMA is going to block this kick."

My good friend Kevin Carden looked skeptical, as did his 92,012 crimson-clad friends. But I, in my neutral green, believed without a shadow of a doubt that Tennessee's game-winning field goal attempt was not going to split the uprights because it was never going to leave the ground. Of course, I didn't really know, and if I actually could predict the future I'd certainly find a more lucrative career, but on the whole, no one has more faith in the Alabama Crimson Tide than Auburn fans.

● ● ●

The game's first half had been fairly boring, unless you happened to be a field-goalaholic. Alabama's Lee Tiffin had kicked three of them, one a fifty-yarder that flew fifty yards and one inch. Tennessee's kicker, Daniel Lincoln, had made one field goal of his own, but he missed a forty-seven-yarder as the half expired, and Alabama went to the locker room with a 9–3 lead.

The bands performed, then cleared the field, and the third quarter began—a quarter that would see neither team do anything worth mentioning. So we went to the fourth with Alabama still leading 9–3.

I personally hate six-point leads. They're better than six-point deficits, but only marginally. With a six-point lead you know you are just one snap away from calamity. People who are comfortable with six-point leads would probably be comfortable letting Michael Vick keep their dogs.

Tennessee had a chance to cut into Alabama's six-point lead when Daniel Lincoln attempted a forty-three-yard field goal five minutes into the fourth quarter, only to have it blocked by Terrence Cody, the Tide's six foot, five inch, 365 lb. defensive tackle. If you'd like to know what it is like to try to kick a field goal over Terrence Cody, walk outside and stand a Volkswagen Bug on its end, and then stand five yards away and try to kick a ball over it. (Actually, if you're the sort of person who can stand a VW on its end, you probably *are* Terrence Cody.)

After the block, Alabama took the ball, marched down the field, and Lee Tiffin slipped another long field goal just over the crossbar to give the Tide a 12–3 lead. Then when Tennessee gave Alabama the ball back with five minutes to play, the game was all but over. Tennessee fans rushed to the exits, as did a few Tide fans who wanted to beat the traffic.[1] But something funny happened on the way to Alabama's eighth win. Mark Ingram, star

---

1. I've never understood the traffic beaters. Is there something going on at their house that is more exciting than the end of an SEC football game? If so, why'd they leave home in the first place?

tailback and late-game workhorse, lost a fumble for the first time in his career.

The Vol offense, which had been stifled all day by the tough Bama D, came alive. And when Jonathan Crompton hit Gerald Jones for an eleven-yard touchdown pass, Alabama's once-comfortable lead was cut from nine to two.

But there were only seventy-nine seconds left. Tennessee's only hope was an onside kick. No one ever recovers onside kicks, until they do, and this night the Vols did. When Crompton hit Luke Stocker on a long pass over the middle, Tennessee found itself at the Alabama twenty-seven-yard line. That's when Tennessee head coach Lane Kiffin started playing for the field goal. I tried not to groan out loud.

Kevin had called me earlier in the week with a free ticket to the game. It belonged to his father-in-law, former Tide star quarterback Gary Rutledge, who was sick with swine flu. I was thankful for the ticket, but felt bad because all week I'd been praying for Bama players to get the swine flu[2] and wondered if perhaps God thought I meant former players.

So really the only problem with the seat, apart from the guilt, was that Gary's season tickets are right in the middle of the former player's section. Now I don't want you to think I'd planned to sit in Bryant-Denny Stadium and openly root against the home team. Sure, as an Auburn fan and SEC West rival, I wanted Alabama to lose, but I was there as a strictly neutral observer.

Neutrality aside, when Lane Kiffin settled on a forty-five-yard field goal, I let out a deep sigh because I knew Alabama had just won the game. I must have been the only person who knew, because all around me I could hear people pleading with the Maker of the universe to come down and alter the path of this

---

2. This is a joke. Please don't return my book.

kick. I turned to Kevin, and he looked like he'd just seen Bear Bryant's ghost, so I put my arm around him and said once again, "You *know* Alabama is going to block this kick."

● ● ●

I'd arrived in Tuscaloosa early that morning, and on the drive over I saw more Tennessee flags than I would have thought possible. But the Vols were coming off a bye week and had spent the previous Saturday teaching the Georgia Bulldogs how to play football. Seems UT fans, who two weeks earlier were too disheartened to even talk about football, now had a confidence bordering on cockiness. Yep, the Big Orange Nation as a whole seemed to have found their swagger. I told you faith can be a fickle thing.

First thing Saturday morning I met Tommy Ford for breakfast at the Tuscaloosa IHOP. Tommy works in the Alabama Athletic Department as the director of donor programs, and is apparently known by every man, woman, and child in town, or at least everyone who frequents this particular IHOP.

I ordered the Football Lover's Combo, which consisted of, I kid you not, eggs, sausage links, hash browns, bacon, and a massive piece of French toast stuffed with cream cheese filling and topped with strawberries and whipped cream. Tommy ordered eggs and coffee, making me feel like a tremendous pig. Actually, eating all my food and then picking at what was left of Tommy's eggs made me feel like a pig, but you know what I mean.

While I attempted to ruin my cardiovascular health, Tommy talked to me about writing. He had written a book about brothers, cousins, and father-son combos that had played for Alabama called *Alabama's Family Tides*, and he was selected to write the *Alabama Football All Access Vault*. If you are an Alabama fan and don't have the *All Access Vault* sitting on your coffee table right now—well, you aren't really an Alabama fan, are you?

Tommy and I both grew up in the same part of the state, and we talked about friends and acquaintances. But Tommy knows people everywhere, and not only that, he knows Alabama fans everywhere. "Do you know Thom Rainer?" he asked me. I did not, and Tommy informed me that Thom is the president and CEO of Lifeway Christian Resources, and he is a big Alabama fan.

"Thom graduated from the university," Tommy said. "He's a big football fan, and he really dislikes Auburn."

Great. I could just picture Thom Rainer reading my bio and slapping one of Lifeway's infamous "Read with Discernment" stickers across the cover of my book.[3] "I'm sure you know Mac Powell, the lead singer of Third Day," Tommy continued.

"He's a Bama fan too?"

"Oh yeah, huge fan. Goes to a lot of games."

Tommy went on to name actors, musicians, dancers, designers, heads of state, *American Idol* judges, and cartoon characters who all cheer for the Crimson Tide.

I was starting to feel defensive, like I should speak up for Auburn somehow, so I blurted out, "Jimmy Buffett went to Auburn for a quarter."

"That's nice," Tommy said, patting me on the head.

It was getting close to 8:00 a.m., and Tommy's game-day duties called, so we said good-bye and I drove to Wal-Mart to buy some Pepto-Bismol. Shockingly, the Football Lover's Combo was not a big hit with my digestive system.

I like going to Wal-Marts in college towns. Wal-Mart is one store that really buys into the whole school spirit thing, oftentimes spelling out the university's name with thousands of soda boxes.

---

3. In 2009 Lifeway began adding stickers to books that "may have espoused thoughts, ideas, or concepts that could be considered inconsistent with historical evangelical theology." I don't know how evangelicals have historically viewed Auburn fans, but I get the feeling I may be in trouble.

The Tuscaloosa Wal-Mart was no different, and I was greeted at the door by a kiosk stacked with houndstooth hats.

The houndstooth thing has exploded in the last five years. Growing up I don't recall ever seeing it at Bama games, but now Bear Bryant's famous black-and-white-check pattern is more prevalent on Saturdays than crimson. You see it on the well-known fedoras, you see it on baseball caps, you see it on women's coats and scarves, and I wouldn't be shocked if some Tuscaloosa churches had made the switch to houndstooth choir robes.

● ● ●

With my stomach settled, I drove over to Alabama's campus for the first time since 2006. Tricia and I had been to the first four Iron Bowls played in Bryant-Denny Stadium but decided to skip the 2008 contest because, well, you didn't have to be an Old Testament prophet to see that disaster coming.

Driving down McFarland Boulevard, I passed Krispy Kreme and the apartment complex I had all but signed a lease at many lifetimes ago. It's weird to look back on the big decisions in your life and imagine how things would have been different had you chosen another path. Had I gone through with my plans to attend the University of Alabama, it's doubtful I would even know half the people in my cell phone. I suppose it's not out of the question that I could've still met my wife, but she had a hard enough time dating a *former* Alabama fan—had I been a graduate we wouldn't have made it past the first date.

I found a parking lot near Fraternity Row that looked reserved, but no one was checking for passes, so I quickly backed in and left the scene. I decided to stop by the BCM to see Billy Jones, an Alabama student I'd spoken with back in the summer. The BCM parking lot was alive with activity as students directed traffic and wedged in as many cars as they could for $20 a pop. They told me all the money went to summer missions, and I felt a little guilty for the parking spot I'd likely just stolen. I asked for Billy and was pointed inside, where he was on Saturday bathroom duty. This isn't as bad as it sounds. Billy's job was basically to greet visitors at the door, and point them to the bathroom when they inevitably asked.

Billy grew up in Michigan. He came to Alabama as part of a package deal for Mark Ingram. Okay, that's a lie. Billy is actually a genius of sorts and is in Tuscaloosa on a full scholarship to study engineering.

We talked a bit about Bama's season so far. The Tide was 7–0, and now ranked number one in the nation for the first time in recent memory. And though Alabama was a prohibitive favorite today against the Vols, Billy seemed a little hesitant to predict a blowout win.

"It'll be a tough game," he told me. "I think we pull away late, but I'm nervous."

Billy then went on to tell me the BCM had already made an initial inquiry into renting a bus to take students to Pasadena for the BCS championship game. So while he wouldn't admit to feeling confident about today's game, he and the rest of the Baptists on campus obviously didn't expect the Tide to lose anytime soon.

I left the BCM and decided to explore the campus to see what had changed. I walked down University Boulevard, past the President's Mansion and Denny Chimes, making my way toward Bryant-Denny Stadium.

In 2006 Alabama expanded its north end zone, adding a third upper deck, and constructing the Walk of Champions outside the stadium. I had only seen photographs of the Walk of Champions and decided to take a look. The sidewalk leading up to the stadium is adorned with carved stones recognizing Alabama's many national and conference championships. Nearer to the stadium are four bronze statues of the men who have led the Crimson Tide to national titles: Wallace Wade, Frank Thomas, Bear Bryant, and Gene Stallings. Behind each statue is a semicircular wall with the years of each coach's respective national championships. But down past the four coaches stands another wall without a statue. It made me think of the apostle Paul's travels to Athens, where he encountered a shrine to the unknown god. When I told an Alabama friend about this he said, "No, that shrine is for Coach Saban—just give him time."

On the south side of Bryant-Denny Stadium, construction cranes soared high above the campus skyline. Another end zone renovation is underway, and when completed Bryant-Denny Stadium will comfortably seat every man, woman, and child in the state of Alabama. After that I suppose it will float around the galaxy and destroy planets.

My sightseeing adventure killed close to an hour, but I still had an eternity before meeting up with Kevin Carden, so I walked back to the quad and took a seat on a bench for some good old-fashioned people watching.

Everyone looked happy. Tailgates were hopping, music was playing, and there was excitement in the air. Obviously, everyone believed the 2009 Crimson Tide was something special, and a thirteenth national championship would soon be theirs. Then out of nowhere a small red elephant appeared on my left shoulder.

"You had their excitement once," the elephant said. "And you could have it again."

Then another poof of smoke, and a small tiger riding an eagle appeared over my right shoulder.

"Don't listen to him. You are part of a family now. The Auburn family. We have something they could never know."

"Who wants to be part of a family," the elephant said, "when you can be part of a nation? The Bama nation!"

"Don't listen to him Chad," the tiger pleaded. "You went to Auburn, and you're an Auburn man!"

"Auburn man." The elephant laughed. "What does that even mean? Look, Chad, go to the bookstore, buy yourself a nice crimson sweatshirt, and get back on board for number thirteen."

"Chad, please, your wife will leave you! It's not worth it!"

"We can find you another wife, Chad. Have you seen the houndstooth twins?"

I was about to start responding to these persuasive talking animals when my phone rang. It was Kevin Carden.

"Hey Chad, we just parked—what are you doing?"

"Uhh, I'm not doing anything," I said, a little too defensively.

"Okay," Kevin said. "Well, if you want we can meet at Denny Chimes in ten minutes."

I found Kevin near the team captain handprints at the base of Denny Chimes. He was with his wife Stacey, and their two-year-old daughter, Hope, who was wearing a T-shirt that read "My Poppy is a Legend, #11" in reference to the flu-stricken Gary Rutledge.

Kevin grew up in Tuscaloosa, the son of a school principal, and he is perhaps the craziest person I know. He is always telling us stories of insane things he and his two brothers did growing up, including rollerblading on the back of a pick-up truck driving sixty miles-per-hour. I'm convinced there were seven or eight Carden brothers, but only three of them lived through childhood.

The four of us walked through the quad to Alabama's Campus Crusade tailgate, where we feasted on a Chick-fil-A nugget tray, and then Kevin introduced me to his friend Jeff Norris, campus director for Bama Crusade.

Jeff's father played at Alabama under Bear Bryant, and he admitted to being a recovering football junkie. "It's a struggle," he told me. "And I'm constantly asking the guys I mentor where they turn to find joy in life. I mean, as Christians we are all pro-grammed to say Jesus, but if I spend ninety minutes a day at BamaOnLine and five minutes in the Bible—well, my actions are speaking pretty loud."

Jeff had hit on something rather close to home: the Internet. I currently belong to four Auburn sports message boards, and if you were to compare the amount of time I've spent reading those boards for the past five years to, oh let's say, the amount of time I've spent reading the Bible, well, it would be embarrassing. The Internet has brought us a lot of great things, like chadgibbs.com, but it has also made it easier to find people as crazy as ourselves, so now we can spend all day talking to them about how awesome whatever we think is awesome is.

A big part of the draw of these boards is they can make you feel like an insider. You are promised you'll know when a recruit commits, or when a player is injured at practice, and it becomes addictive. I find myself checking the boards constantly, wondering if something has changed in the ten minutes since I last checked. I mean what if a four-star lineman commits, and I don't learn about it that minute? The world would end, right?

● ● ●

Shortly before kickoff I finally got the text I'd been waiting for. It was from Hunter Johnson, who said he and some friends were at Galettes, the closest bar to Bryant-Denny Stadium. I walked down and Hunter met me outside. He was wearing a crimson sports coat over a white shirt with a crimson and white striped tie. A crimson and white striped belt held up his khaki pants over the tops of his crimson and white sneakers. In his pocket was the cigar he planned to smoke once the Tide had disposed of the Volunteers.

"So you're a Barner?" Hunter asked me point blank.

"Yeah, I went to Auburn," I told him.

"I thought so," he said. "But it was hard to tell because your website doesn't have a bunch of Aubie crap on it."

"Thanks, I guess. You know, I did grow up an Alabama fan."

"What? Why? How could you go to Auburn?"

"I just did," I told him. "I think in the end it's where God wanted me."

"Whatever," Hunter said with a smile. "I've never seen any evidence of the Holy Spirit in Lee County."

I liked Hunter immediately. He's one of those rare guys that can make you laugh even when he's making fun of you.

Hunter's mom works in the Crimson Tide athletic department, and he told me what it was like growing up around the program. "I was indoctrinated at a young age. I'd be visiting my mom at work, and Coach Stallings would invite me into his office, and we'd drink Coke and eat cheese puffs and watch film. From there, it was pretty much impossible for me not to become a fanatic."

Almost anticipating a great answer, I asked Hunter if his passion for all things Crimson had ever got him in trouble, maybe made him say something he later regretted. "Oh definitely," he said. "During the 2004 Iron Bowl, Alabama had an injured player, so the Auburn team huddled up to pray for him. The entire stadium was dead silent, and I screamed out from the student section, 'I don't know who you're praying to, but it isn't God!' I got some pretty rough looks from the people sitting around me."

Hunter's outburst, while slightly hilarious, was appalling and deserving of the mean looks he received. But had it been posted on a message board, it would have been par for the course, and that is where I think the anonymity poses a major problem. I'm looking at a photograph of our wedding party right now, and there are five Alabama graduates, and I love them all. But when we get on these message boards, we start to talk about fans of our rival like they were Nazis. Say one kind word about a rival school's fans, and you run the risk of being labeled a traitor. And no one wants that because then someone might withhold insider information from you. So we say awful things, and we read the awful things they say about us, and eventually we start to believe all these things. I'll see an Alabama fan in the mall, and I'll think of something AubieHater1985 posted. Then I start to think that shopper must hate me because all the Bama fans on the Internet do, so I start to hate them back. And when you think everyone you see in a crimson shirt hates you, it makes the outcome of a football game seem that much more important.

I wanted to stay and talk to Hunter a little longer since he probably had dozens of stories just as bad as that one, but kickoff was near, so we said good-bye and went to our respective seats in Bryant-Denny Stadium.

● ● ●

"You don't know that," Kevin said, looking sicker by the second.

"Trust me, Alabama is going to block this kick."

The nervous crowd rose as one when Tennessee placekicker Daniel Lincoln trotted out onto the field. Terrence Cody, the mountain of a man who had blocked the earlier field goal, stood over the ball, encouraging the Alabama nation to make as much noise as they possibly could. The ball was snapped, and the stadium seemed extremely loud and incredibly quiet all at once. You heard the thump of the kick, then you heard a louder thump when the ball met the massive left hand of Terrence Cody.

Then you couldn't hear anything at all.

Bryant-Denny Stadium was engulfed in a sea of crimson madness that swirled around one stoic soul in a green shirt. And when Kevin finished singing the last chorus of "Rammer Jammer," he turned to me and said, "Never a doubt."

● ● ●

Leaving the stadium, Kevin seemed to be in a reflective mood. The decade had been a long one for Alabama fans, and I think maybe he was feeling a little emotional about the win. "You know," he began, "when I moved to Birmingham and met all of you Auburn guys, you really made me feel like crap. Y'all had the big winning streak over us, and whenever the conversations turned to football, I would leave feeling everything in my life, my home, my degree, my car, was inferior to yours just because your college had a winning streak over mine."

At first I felt guilty, and I tried to reevaluate the way I'd treated Kevin in the past. But I'd always treated him great. Sure we joke about football, but not in a mean way. I think Kevin was just projecting those feelings onto whatever we said. I say this because as Kevin and I talked, I began to feel like everything in *my* life was inferior to his because his team was now 8–0, and number one in the land.

● ● ●

That night I stayed with April and Jonathan Hollingsworth. Jonathan was my college roommate, and he is now a golf course superintendent in Tuscaloosa. We both went to Auburn as Alabama fans, but he only spent two years on the Plains, and even then he drove home most weekends to see April. So unlike yours truly, Jonathan never had a conversion experience, and he couldn't wait to talk about Mount Cody when I walked in the door.

I listened to Jonathan's recap of the game I'd just seen, then asked if he would turn on the Auburn–LSU game. When LSU went up 24–0, I asked if he would turn it off, then I excused myself to the guest bedroom.

If only I could see days like this coming. I'd go play golf or work at a soup kitchen or do anything but sit and watch ten hours of soul-crushing football. Laying there, staring at the ceiling, I felt a creeping dread. It was a feeling that is hard to explain, but it left me not wanting to go forward. I didn't want to go to church in the morning. I didn't want to face my workweek and all the Bama fans I would certainly encounter. I didn't want to do any of it, because I wanted to curl up in a ball and have someone wake me when the season was over. When I heard the Hollingsworths go to bed, I slipped outside and called Tricia.

"Hey," I said.

"Hey," she replied.

We just sat there, not saying anything for what seemed like hours. Auburn had lost three games in a row, and Alabama looked like they would never lose again. "You know," I said, finally breaking the silence. "I don't even want to write this stupid book anymore."

"I know," Tricia said. And we said good night.

●　●　●

The next morning I went to church with the Hollingsworths at Open Door Baptist Church in Northport, just outside of Tuscaloosa. Keith Pugh is the lead pastor at Open Door; he also played wide receiver for Alabama during the Bryant years, which meant I wasn't particularly interested in hearing anything he had to say that morning. Fortunately Rev. Pugh was not preaching; unfortunately Brian Payne, another former Tide player, was, so I sank back into my own despair, trying to close out the crimson world around me.

This is what I've been talking about, and I don't mean getting upset about a football loss. We're southerners, for crying out loud, and southerners are passionate people. Of course I'm going to feel pain when Auburn loses and joy when they win. There are times, however, like today, when the disappointment carries over into the next day and the next. If I see a disappointing movie on

Saturday night, I'm not going to let it keep me from worshiping God the next morning. So why do I let a football loss ruin my entire week? Both are for my entertainment. Why have I made one life or death? Maybe these were the questions God wanted me to reflect on.

So that's what I did while Brian Payne preached what I'm sure was an excellent sermon. And do you know what I realized? I really don't like football that much.

Seriously.

I mean, obviously I *like* it, but the amount of time, money, and energy I put into football seems disproportionate to how much I truly care about the sport. What I like is the way I feel about myself when Auburn is winning games. So much of my self-image comes from my affiliation with a football team, and when my team isn't winning, I feel like a failure. Conversely, when Auburn is rolling, I'm the most confident, joyous person you could meet. Factor in the rivalry, which has its ugliest aspects magnified by the Internet, and it's no wonder the games feel so important to me. In my mind, I am my team. My worth as a person is in direct proportion to the success Auburn is having on the field. And for a child of God to think his worth as a person has anything to do with a game played by college students is utterly terrifying.

So sitting there, while Brian Payne preached on God knows what, I kept saying to myself over and over, "I am not my team. I am not my team."

"But, Chad, you are a vital part of the Auburn family," said the little tiger on my shoulder.

"Come back to the Tide," said the little red elephant. "Another title is just around the corner."

"Why don't you just shut up for once," I said. "Both of you."

UNIVERSITY OF KENTUCKY

OCTOBER 31, 2009

Hit hard; remember the Bible says, "It's better to give than to receive."

Adolph Rupp

UNIVERSITY OF KENTUCKY junior Bryan Taylor holds the dubious distinction of being the first SEC fan I spoke to while working on this book. In his email he spoke about how excited he was to "find another person who loves both sports and the Lord." He also called me "Mr. Gibbs," and I decided we had to talk, if for no other reason than to tell him not to call me that again.

Bryan was in Birmingham for the summer, interning at UAB Hospital. He is a biology major pursuing a career in physical therapy for sports injuries. I'm glad there are people out there who can do that stuff, because when I see an injury on television, I have trouble eating the rest of the day.

We decided to meet at McAlister's Deli and did that awkward thing you do when meeting someone you've never seen where one of you pulls out a cell phone, calls a number, then looks around for someone to answer. Bryan was standing right beside me, so we said hello. He was a handsome, athletic-looking kid who obviously could destroy me in any competition involving strength, speed, or hand-eye coordination, though I might hold my own in darts.

Bryan was very receptive to my ideas, which was all the endorsement I needed. He shared some of his own struggles with the idol of sports and said he thought his involvement in FCA had helped him gain perspective. He told me he would be taking part in the Big Blue Bible Drive, an initiative headed by Gavin Duerson, UK's FCA director, with the goal of placing a Bible in the hands of every scholarship athlete on UK's campus. I'd love to see Auburn do this—only partly because I'm convinced it would help us win games.

My schedule took me to Lexington the weekend Kentucky was playing Mississippi State. I knew most SEC eyes would be turned to Jacksonville, where Georgia and Florida were meeting in the game formerly known as the World's Largest Outdoor Cocktail Party. After that, most folks would be following the Tennessee–South Carolina game, in which the Vols would wear black jerseys for the first—and hopefully last—time. Since I wasn't going to be at the marquee game of the day, I had a bright idea: why not ask Kentucky for a press pass?

I went online to see if this was even possible and found a link from the media guide to a website Kentucky and most other schools use to process media credentials. The site was full of legal mumbo jumbo, and after trying to read through it, I began to worry that not only would I not be issued a press pass, but I would somehow get in trouble for even trying. But I decided it probably wasn't a felony, so I hit submit and immediately forgot I'd even applied.

Months later, only a few days before I was set to leave for Lexington, I received the following email:

Chad, back in August, you requested a credential for the Kentucky – Mississippi State game as a freelance author. Are you still interested in coming to the game? What kind of project do you have?

Tony Neely
Media Relations Director
University of Kentucky Athletics

I called Tony within seconds of receiving his email and said yes, of course I still wanted media credentials. He asked about the book, and I explained what I was doing, praying Tony wasn't an angry atheist who went into media relations in order to crush young Christian writers. Thankfully, Tony said my pass would be waiting at media will-call, and he'd see me on Saturday. I hung up the phone and began dancing around my office. I was now a member of the press, just like Geraldo.

Brian Marshall, the campus minister for Christian Student Fellowship, put me in touch with John Biery, a UK senior. John and I spoke during the week, and I asked if there would be anything going on Friday night we could attend.

"Oh yes," he replied. "Lexington has the world's largest 'Thriller' reenactment every year on the Friday before Halloween."

"Of course you do."

You see in the South we like to reenact things—particularly Civil War battles and occasionally Michael Jackson videos. I searched for "Lexington + Thriller" on YouTube, and sure enough, hundreds of people take to the street, stumble around like zombies, then break out into choreographed dance, as the living dead are prone to do. As a child I couldn't watch that video; the King of Pop's crazy yellow eyes gave me nightmares, and I wasn't particularly thrilled about seeing it in person twenty years later.

I asked John if perhaps the Christian Student Fellowship had something less scary going on.

"Sure," he said. "I think our Geek Ministry has something going on that night."

I laughed. "You mean Greek Ministry right? Like fraternities and sororities."

"No," John said. "I mean *geek*. Like kids who play World of Warcraft."

I couldn't tell if John was joking or not, so I went to CSF's website, and sure enough, there was a page for the Geek Ministry:

Are you a gamer? Do you have a plan mapped out in the event of the inevitable zombie apocalypse? Have you ever dressed up as Boba Fett for Halloween? Or just because you wanted to? If you answered yes to any of these questions (or even if you didn't), then CSF is where you need to be.

Come participate in video game tournaments, watch your favorite movies and shows, and discuss the latest and greatest in tech and gaming while growing closer to Jesus in community.

I'm admittedly a *Star Wars* freak—one of those fans who will never forgive George Lucas for making Greedo shoot first—so the Geek Ministry sounded like something I'd be all about.

In the end, however, I decided not to leave for Lexington until Saturday morning. I'd like to blame the delay on John Biery's Facebook profile, which was full of references to skullets, a hairstyle similar to a mullet, only with a shaved head on top. Just imagine Ben Franklin in a tank top. And John's photo page was full of pictures of people sporting skullets, including John himself. It sort of scared me, but I do live in Alabama, so it's not like skullets aren't something I see every day.

I'd also like to blame the delay on my devotion to my marriage. These trips were starting to wear on me a bit, and with Tricia's crazy work schedule, we were hardly seeing each other. She was actually off that Friday night, so if I waited until Saturday to leave, we'd get to spend some time together.

The truth is slightly more embarrassing. It had been a long week at work. I'd vowed to stay off the message boards, but couldn't help myself, and what I read only made me feel worse about Auburn's sudden collapse. Worse than that, it looked like Alabama was on a God-ordained march to their thirteenth national title. My heart would race just thinking about it. I'm not sure what I thought would happen to me if Alabama won the national championship, but I knew it would be bad. Because if you turn to football for self-worth, then having your rival win it all must make you worthless, right? So I stayed home on Friday night and sulked, because the truth is I'm a big baby that takes football way too seriously.

But when my alarm went off at 3:30 the following morning, I began to think staying home Friday night to pout might have been a mistake. The drive from Birmingham to Lexington takes about six hours, and you lose an hour when you cross into the Eastern Time Zone. The morning was foggy, though, honestly, there isn't much to look at until you reach the Blue Grass Parkway, which is a beautiful stretch of highway full of horse farms and whisky distilleries. Close to Lexington I pulled over to fill up my tank, and walking inside to pay, I passed a man wearing an Auburn cap.

"War Eagle," I said.

He gave me the strangest look and muttered an awkward "Thanks."

SEC fans are a little cultish, and battle cries are considered a perfectly acceptable form of greeting, even if the person you are talking to is a complete stranger. However, sometimes you run across a person, like my new friend at this Kentucky gas station, who buys team hats because the colors are cool. These encounters are weird for everyone involved.[1] When I finally pulled into town,

---

1. Not as awkward as the time a man shouted "War Eagle" at me at the Holocaust Museum. Of course, I did wear an Auburn T-shirt to the Holocaust Museum, so perhaps I should shoulder some of the blame.

I called Billy Fry, a crazy Cats fan I met through a mutual friend from Auburn. When Billy heard I was scheduled to visit Lexington in November, he lambasted me, saying it was a rookie mistake not to come in October when I could spend some time at Keeneland, which he referred to as "God's Playground." I had no clue what Keeneland could be, so I Googled it.

Keeneland, it turns out, is a horse track. Not only that, it is a world-renowned horse track that was voted number one in the country by the Horseplayers Association of North America. Races are only run twice a year, in April and October, and when I called Billy to let him know my schedule had changed, he was thrilled and agreed to be my official guide to Keeneland.

After driving through rain and fog for nearly seven hours, I finally arrived at Billy Fry's home and was greeted in the driveway by an attractive dark-haired woman with an accent I couldn't quite place. "Hallo, I'm Mariska," she said, and invited me inside. Mariska looked and talked like the kind of girls who are always getting James Bond into trouble, so I was apprehensive about doing anything she told me. Nonetheless, I followed her in, and she introduced me to Billy, who was in the kitchen putting some finishing touches on his award-winning BBQ pork.

Billy explained to me that Mariska was his girlfriend, her accent was South African, and if she had wanted to kill me, she would've probably done it in the driveway. This was somewhat comforting.

Billy told me his family had held Kentucky football season tickets since before Commonwealth Stadium was built. "My dad prides himself on having never left a game early. It's sad but true. He hasn't been to all the games, though, and was fortunate enough to miss the Bluegrass Miracle." Billy was referring to the 2002 Kentucky–LSU game, where the Wildcats lost on a seventy-four-yard Hail Mary as time expired. The Kentucky students rushed the field as the pass was thrown and had already torn down one goalpost by the time they realized LSU had won the game.

"Were you there for that game?" I asked him.

"Yes. It sucked."

Billy told me about his faith growing up. "Mom is Southern Baptist and Dad is Catholic. Mom went to Mass with us until I was about sixteen years old, when she looked over during one particularly boring homily to see me, my dad, and my brother all dozing off. She figured if we didn't care about the church we were raised in, why should she, so she bailed. Not out of our life, just on over to Lexington Avenue Baptist Church."

I laughed and asked where he went to church now.

"I'm not much of a church man myself," he said. "But I do appreciate studying religion as a subject, rather than a zealot. I actually lived in Israel for a summer on an archaeological dig. But if you want, I can take you to the Catholic church I grew up in. Better yet, I have a line on a snake-handling church in Lancaster, if you want to try it. I haven't been, but my friend could probably get us in. They are pretty leery of strangers though, so we must be careful. And I hear it's a pretty long service, at least two and a half hours, and my friend said when he went, they stood for over an hour straight."

This was enticing, but I'd already spoken to some nice people at a church in Lexington, and I'd have hated to tell them they lost out because they don't incorporate snakes into worship. Besides, I kept thinking how mad Tricia would be if I died from what would amount to a self-inflicted snakebite wound.

While Billy told stories, the Auburn–Ole Miss game kicked off, and early on the Tigers were holding their own, which was surprising to everyone after three straight losses. At the end of the first quarter we left for Keeneland, and I was shocked to see how many people were out tailgating at the track. It finally dawned on me that this was kind of a big deal. We pulled up to the valet and Billy pointed out the Clubhouse, a private viewing area he occasionally gets to visit, though not today, especially since my jeans and T-shirt violated every line of the dress code.

Billy bought a program that gave us information on each horse in each race. The statistics were probably helpful if you actually knew what they meant, but I did not, so I had to find an alternative way to bet.

"Hey, where do I know that guy from?"

"That's Calvin Borel. He won the Kentucky Derby and the Preakness last year."

It *was* Calvin Borel, perhaps the only jockey in the world I would recognize. I put $2 on Calvin and his horse to win, and we walked outside to watch the race.

At first you can't really see the horses, so you keep up with them on the massive video screen in the infield. But soon they make the last turn, and people start jumping and shouting in hopes the particular horse they bet on is inspired by noise. It's addicting, no doubt, seeing your horse come down the stretch with a two-length lead. But when he fades late to finish third, you learn screaming "Calvin Borel should be turned into glue" is generally frowned upon at Keeneland.

In the end I only lost $14 in two hours at Keeneland, so financially it was no different than seeing Avatar, and here my head wasn't hurting. Billy finished in the red as well, but Mariska pocketed close to twenty bucks. Of course, Dr. No was probably telling her which horses to bet on.

Back at Billy's we turned on the Auburn game, which was tied at last report, only to see Auburn had reeled off twenty-one points in less than five minutes to lead Ole Miss 31 – 7. It was now official; this was the strangest football season ever.

Billy's friend Kelly Holderman met us at the house, and the four of us loaded up the car and drove to Commonwealth Stadium. During the short trip I explained my book to Holderman, and the topic inevitably led to a conversation about Tim Tebow. "He's great and all," Holderman said. "But don't you find it odd he spent the summer in Africa castrating children?"

"What?!" Billy and I said in unison.

"Tebow was in Africa all summer castrating little African babies."

"I think he was *circumcising* them," Billy said, choking back the laughter.

"No, I'm pretty sure he was castrating them."

Kentucky's Commonwealth Stadium is tucked into the southeastern edge of campus. Tailgating, best I could tell, is done mostly in the massive parking lots surrounding the stadium. This is much more practical than having people set up tents all over the campus, but it doesn't quite feel right. It feels too ... *NFL*. That being said, Billy's friends have a great spot—maybe a pooch punt away from the stadium entrance—so I got over the fact we weren't on grass pretty quickly.

After a quick check of the Big Green Egg, Billy said we had about an hour before the BBQ was ready, so I took a walk around the stadium to meet John Biery and apologized for not coming up Friday night.

John was, thankfully, no longer sporting the skullet from his Facebook profile.

"So what was the deal with that?" I asked.

John just laughed. "It was a contest Christian Student Fellowship put on last year to see who could grow the best mullet. I won."

"I'm sure."

"And then when we left for our mission trip to Africa, I had to take it up a notch, so I went for the skullet."

How beautiful is the skullet of him who brings good news.

John's story was familiar. He prefers to worship on Saturday nights at Southland Christian Church in Lexington, "but if Kentucky plays late on Saturdays, I settle for the Sunday service." He joked about telling his childhood minister the crime rate in Boston had just doubled because the Celtics had drafted a player from his minister's alma mater. "And I was only eleven years old," John added. "And I know I ride some of the Louisville fans on campus a little too hard. It probably voids my witness a bit. But there are just too many of them on this campus and it infuriates me a bit."

I laughed because I was once the rival fan on an enemy campus. This alone should give me perspective I seem to be lacking, but instead I talk about it like a religious conversion. It wasn't, you know. I just started cheering for a different school's football team. That's it. The angels didn't sing. I doubt they even noticed. I could start cheering for another school tomorrow; fans do it all the time. It seems like a pretty arbitrary thing to garner self-worth from, but alas.

I wished John good luck and told him we'd certainly come back to Lexington next season when Auburn plays at Kentucky. To make things interesting, I told him if Kentucky could win consecutive games over Auburn for the first time ever, Tricia would grow a skullet.

The end of the tailgate meant it was time to pick up my media pass. But what if I asked for my pass the wrong way — would they know I was only a pretend journalist and refuse me entry? So I stood around the corner and watched a few real members of the press to see how they did things, then cautiously followed suit.

I must admit having a press pass around my neck felt glorious. I stood around for a few minutes, pretending to make phone calls and looking important, but when no one stopped to ask for my autograph, I decided to go down to the field.

Stepping onto an SEC field during pregame warm-ups was one of the highlights of my fall. There is just so much going on. Players are stretching, coaches are yelling, and the band is lining up for its pregame show. I stood there, soaking it all in, occasionally looking to the stands and wondering, "Why are all the Kentucky fans wearing black?"

"We were supposed to have a blackout tonight," Billy Fry told me after the game. "The team was going to wear black jerseys and everything, but late in the process Coach Brooks said no. I guess that's what happens when your team is coached by a curmudgeon."

Just before kickoff I made my way up to the press box, where I met Tony Neely, the man responsible for press credentials. Tony, it turns out, is also a believer, and he told me how excited he was about my book. Then he showed me where I'd be sitting and pointed me to the break room, where I had access to all the food I could eat. As I ate my fifth ice cream sandwich, I thought, *Journalism rules.*

The game was great. Kentucky led 10–3 after the first quarter, and I made my way back to the field to watch the game up close. I was standing near the goal line when Kentucky picked off a Bulldog pass on fourth and goal, and the explosion of noise made me cower in fear. That's when I realized *all* SEC stadiums are loud.

Kentucky took a 17–10 lead to the half, and I went back to the press box for more food. (Read: ice cream sandwiches.) From there I watched what became the Anthony Dixon show. Mississippi State's tailback would finish the night with a school-record 252 yards, giving his Bulldogs a 31–24 lead late in the game.

The Wildcats took possession with just under six minutes to play, and freshman quarterback Morgan Newton led them down the field. Newton had been forced into action by injury and perhaps was not yet capable of running the entire offense. But every time Kentucky offensive coordinator and head-coach-in-waiting

Joker Phillips ran a conservative play, fans below would turn toward the press box and scream insults in Joker's direction. This was awkward, because some of the coach's wives were in the box between the press and the coaches. I wanted to walk over and tell them, "It's not what you think, ladies—they're actually telling your husbands to go to *Hail*. It's a town in Kentucky, and there are probably some good recruits there."

The game ended when Newton took a sack on fourth down at the State sixteen-yard line. Fans turned and screamed at Joker, then left the stadium sullen. But as of this writing, the Big Blue men's basketball team is once again a national powerhouse, so I imagine most have gotten over this loss already.

After the game I was able to sit in while actual media members interviewed Kentucky head coach Rich Brooks. I thought about asking a question, but then I remembered David Wells's story about Phil Fulmer's wrath, so I chickened out. However, there was more free food in the interview room, and I didn't chicken out of that.

Later I met up with Billy, his brother John, and Holderman. The three of them were upset and drowning their sorrows in what could best be described as moonshine. They lamented a few bad calls, talked about a couple of unlucky breaks, but Billy finally stopped and said, "You know what? This actually worked out perfect for you."

"How so?" I asked.

"This," he said, motioning to all the people griping about the loss. "This is Kentucky football."

● ● ●

The next morning I had breakfast with Nate Collier, a 2004 Kentucky graduate and current seminary student on staff at Broadway Christian Church in downtown Lexington. Nate was not only a solid Christian, but a walking almanac of UK sports. He used to write a blog that may be the only one in America that talks about both Kentucky recruiting and the authority of Scripture.

"Losses are tough," Nate told me. "But as I've gotten older, my perspective has improved." I asked him if football losses were as hard to stomach as basketball ones, and he said, "No, basketball is much tougher, because we aren't used to losing those. This should probably tell you all you need to know. I've seen Kentucky lose to every football team in the league at Commonwealth Stadium, and I've seen us beat every team in the league at Rupp Arena."

Different strokes for different folks I guess, but we all have things in our lives that become too important. Had I been born a Kentucky coal miner's daughter, football losses might not bother me the way they do now, but substituting basketball doesn't make it better. In fact there are three times as many basketball games in a season, so it would probably be worse.

I followed Nate to church that morning at Broadway, a beautiful 140-year-old church in downtown Lexington. The pastor, Phil Ling, reminded me a little of Jim Cramer, the *Mad Money* guy on CNBC, except Rev. Ling didn't roll up his sleeves and scream *booyah!* when I sold my shares of GM. He did, however, give a hard time to Shake Anderson, a visiting musician who happened to be a Louisville fan. Rev. Ling asked Shake's wife about her allegiances, and when she said "Big Blue all the way," Rev. Ling jokingly told her it was a shame Shake couldn't spend eternity with her.

I was feeling pretty good about things when I left the service at Broadway and drove home past horse farms and miles of white fences. The last week's depression had faded with time, though Auburn's surprise win didn't hurt. And it was nice that Bama had an off week, which at least got their predestined national title out of my mind for a little while. But I still needed answers, and at least now I thought I was asking the right questions. I'd wasted so much time looking for a one-size-fits-all formula that would teach me the proper relationship between God and sports, but that formula does not exist. It's something we all have to work out for ourselves, in light of our relationship with God. If something is becoming a hindrance to that relationship, and football certainly was for me, then it needs to be examined. When I started to look closely, I learned that I didn't think nearly as much of myself as God did. God thinks I'm worth sacrificing his Son for, and he thinks that even when Auburn goes 5–7.

It was about time I started to figure out a few things. The season only had four weeks left. And down the stretch we come.

UNIVERSITY OF ARKANSAS

NOVEMBER 7, 2009

Football is only a game. Spiritual things are eternal. Nevertheless, beat Texas.

> *Church sign in Arkansas prior to the 1969*
> *Arkansas–Texas "Game of the Century"*

OKAY CLASS, put up your books and take out a no. 2 pencil—it's pop quiz time.

1. Which school is farthest away from the Southeastern Conference headquarters in Birmingham, Alabama?
   A. Purdue University
   B. Indiana University
   C. University of Arkansas
   D. University of Cincinnati

2. In the last decade, which school defeated Auburn in football by the embarrassing margins of 25, 21, 21, and 17?

A. University of Florida
B. University of Arkansas
C. University of Tennessee
D. University of Alabama

3. Finally, which school was I least looking forward to
   visiting once the 2009 season began?
   A. University of Arkansas
   B. University of Arkansas
   C. University of Arkansas
   D. All of the above

If you answered the University of Arkansas for all three questions, then congratulations, you win a free trip to Fayetteville, Arkansas, courtesy of my publisher, Zondervan.[1] Now before my friends from the Natural State start composing angry emails, please understand my dread had nothing to do with you as people. It's just that over the years the University of Arkansas, when compared to other SEC schools, has brought a disproportionate amount of sorrow into my life. That, and Fayetteville, as Lou Holtz once said, "Isn't the end of the world, but you can see it from there."

Looking back, I realize a great deal of my trepidation revolved around a false belief that Fayetteville was a fourteen-hour drive from Birmingham.

"I guess it could take fourteen hours," said my friend Chris, "the way you drive. But even if you drive the speed limit, you'll be there in less than nine hours."

It's true I drive slowly, and on a long road trip, when I'm likely to get bored and lose focus on the task at hand, I'm prone to drive even slower. This is the reason I have never received a speeding ticket, and why everything seems farther away than it is.

---

1. Editor's Note: We are sorry; there are no free trips to Arkansas. Chad really should have checked with us first.

Of course, at 550 miles, the University of Arkansas *is* a long way from Birmingham. In fact, distance-wise it would've made just as much sense for the SEC to have added Ohio State during its 1992 expansion. Then again, Arkansas folks do at least say "y'all," so I guess the league knew what it was doing.

I felt even better after talking to Jordan Green, my Pac-10 friend, who told me how bad it could've been.

"You realize," he told me, "that if you were writing this book about the Pac-10 and you lived in Tempe, Arizona, you'd have a twenty-four-and-a-half-hour drive to see the University of Washington in Seattle."

"Yeah," I said. "But if I were writing that book, I'd have to call it *Xenu and Football: Scientology and Missed Tackles in the Pac-10.*"

"Shut up."

● ● ●

Even though the trip wasn't nearly as long as I'd feared, I decided to break up the first part and spend Thursday night in Memphis with our good friends Lauren and Nick Rachel. Nick was in Tricia's med school class at the University of South Alabama, and he's now an orthopedic surgery resident on the banks of the Mississippi. Not literally on the banks, since that would put his patients at a high risk for infection, but right near them. Nick's wife, Lauren, is an actress and holds the distinction of performing the finest karaoke version of "Eye of the Tiger" ever.

We ate dinner at Central BBQ, and when our postmeal conversation turned to football, I told Nick and Lauren about the eight trips I'd made so far. Lauren is an Ole Miss grad, and she began making suggestions of things I should do two weeks later when my journeys took me to Oxford. Nick went to undergrad and medical school at USA in Mobile but is a big fan of the Crimson Tide.

"You know he's never even set foot in Tuscaloosa," Lauren told me.

"Wait, you've never been to an Alabama game?" I asked.

"No," he said.

"He hasn't even been to the city," Lauren added.

"Why don't you just cheer for Ole Miss?" I asked. "You've been to dozens of games now with Lauren, and you are going to be going to them for the rest of your life."

"Because I want to be an Alabama fan," Nick said. "Leave me alone."

"But it makes no sense! You grew up three hours away and never even visited?"

"Stop yelling at me."

"Okay," I said. "But I'm going to make fun of you in my book."

● ● ●

The next morning I drove west from Memphis, entering the state of Arkansas for the first time in my life. I'm not really sure how to describe that part of the world. What's an antonym for awe inspiring? I'm not trying to sound mean here. I'm sure the people who live in this part of the world are wonderful, and the land is probably perfect for farming or something, but the drive from Memphis to Little Rock is the traveling equivalent of watching a documentary on the history of boring documentaries.

Once you leave Little Rock, which I did in a hurry, you slowly climb into the Ozarks for what has to be the prettiest three hours of interstate highway in the SEC. I'm talking mountains, lakes, forests, streams, and a massive cooling tower from a nuclear power plant. Okay, so the cooling tower probably wouldn't make it into the Thomas Kinkade painting, but it did have some lights on top he would like.

At last I topped a final hill to see the city of Fayetteville, shining like a hog tusk in the noonday sun. I drove along the outskirts of campus to the First Christian Church, where I met Cheryl Sybrant, the church secretary. When I first emailed, Cheryl suggested I stop by the church office to take a look at the planning calendar. "There are literally yellow Post-it notes on every Saturday during football season," she told me, "just as a reminder of when we might not want to plan a church event."

I said in the introduction that churches have to plan around football, but standing there looking at this calendar, I realized that is not quite right. Churches plan around their members, and their members plan around football. I laughed about it earlier, but when I realize my church doesn't try to serve the community in the fall because they know I won't be there, well, it isn't quite as funny.

Cheryl said, "I'm sure Pastor Pheiffer could give you some insight as well, but you'd have to take it with a grain of salt. He's a TCU Horned Frog."

I figured if a TCU fan and an Auburn fan started talking football, one of us would have an aneurism when the conversation eventually turned to the BCS. So I passed and wished Cheryl a nice day.

● ● ●

Later that afternoon I drove to the home of Jordan Difani, an Arkansas senior and member of Beta Upsilon Chi, the Christian social fraternity also known as Brothers Under Christ or BYX.

Jordan's house was easy to find, considering it had a seven-foot razorback painted above the porch. I walked inside and was greeted by close to a dozen BYX brothers in the living room. Jordan was going to show me around campus and take me to eat some fine Fayetteville grub, but not before I watched a video of BYX dominating last year's UA step show. Their routine was ten minutes of fast-paced awesomeness, and it made me regret being born with the rhythm of a houseplant.

We decided to eat on Dickson Street, the heart of Fayetteville, and chose the Hog Haus Brewing Company—the only operating brewery in northwest Arkansas. I ordered something called the Beer Cheeseburger, which despite sounding gross was actually a delicious burger smothered in white cheese dip. Wait, that still sounds kind of gross, doesn't it?

Over dinner, Jordan and I talked about BYX, which now has close to 160 members at Arkansas, making it a large fraternity by any standard. "We have a lot of great guys," Jordan told me. "And they have interests all over the map."

This was obvious after spending just a few minutes with a handful of brothers. "But what about football?" I asked.

"Oh yeah, we'll have some guys painting up for the game tomorrow."

"And you?"

Jordan laughed. "I won't be painted up, but I'm a big fan. I even went to Dallas earlier this season for the Texas A&M game."

"And does it ever get too big in your life? Any regrets?"

"Sure, sometimes I get really frustrated at the refs or our coach and say things I wish I could take back. You know what I mean?"

Of course I do, and the frustration comes from not having control over the situation. We use all sorts of things to add meaning to our lives, and sports may be the worst. If you thought having a new BMW would give your life purpose, you could work hard and buy the car. Sure, you'd probably be let down, but at least you were in control of the purchase. With sports, we depend on them for significance, but the decisions made on the field are not our own. Coaches call bad plays, referees make bad calls, and there is nothing we can do about it, because it has nothing to do with us in the first place. No wonder we get frustrated and shout things we later regret.

● ● ●

The next morning I drove to campus, where Arkansas was hosting South Carolina, and kickoff was set for 11:30, the most dreaded time in sports. Most SEC fans agree football should never be played before 2:00 p.m., and the fact that some games now start *before* 11:30 is proof we live in a fallen world.

Jordan gave me the names of some guys to talk to that morning, and I went to meet them at the student gate, where a line had formed the night before. It was only 7:45, and freezing, so of course these four guys were shirtless, getting the word *PIGS* painted across their chests.

I was never a chest painter in college. With a painted chest, you want to be on the lowest row of the stadium so cameras can easily pick you out. But on the lowest row you can't really see the game, which was always my reason for going. (Incidentally, from now on I'm going to assume that every shirtless student at a sporting event with a letter painted on his chest is a Christian. I base this on the fact that nearly every campus ministry I contacted over the summer told me about the perfect person for my book, and that person was always a chest painter.)

Back to the four shirtless pigs. Their names were Spencer, Steve, Chris, and David. I talked to Spencer while a girl painstakingly painted an *I* on his chest. He is a member of Century United Methodist in Fayetteville, and a BYX pledge. His older brother, Bryce, was one of the original chest painters, which makes Spencer part of an honorable family legacy, and by honorable I mean slightly embarrassing.

Before entering the stadium, I decided to make a giant lap around Razorback Stadium. Behind the south end zone are two 100-yard practice fields, and behind them sits a massive indoor practice facility. I walked over to take a look, and since the doors weren't locked, I decided to investigate.

Known as the Walker Family Training Center, the 38,000-

square-foot training facility is 110 yards long and houses Arkansas' state-of-the-art indoor football practice field. The building was amazing, and what's more amazing is every school in the league has something similar. It's part of what is being called the SEC Recruiting Arms Race, a spending contest aimed at convincing seventeen-year-old kids to pursue their bachelor's degree at your school. I have mixed feelings about these facilities. When I dream about winning the lottery, which is more often than I like to admit, I like to think of all the great things I would do with my newfound wealth. One of my first acts of hypothetical philanthropy always involves giving a great deal of money to Auburn's athletic department. Not building wells in Africa, and not supporting hundreds of missionaries around the world. No, I dream of paying for a football practice facility to replace the one we built ten years ago, because it always has to be bigger, better, and newer.

Leaving the weight room, I noticed a group of people congregating around a cage, so I went to take a look. Inside the cage was Tusk II, Arkansas's 475-lb. razorback hog. I was able to get pretty close to the cage, and for a moment I was face to face with the scariest thing I've ever seen. Much scarier than Mike, LSU's live tiger. Both animals would kill and eat you if you stumbled upon them in the wild. But with the tiger, at least you know it would be with teeth and claws, and over relatively quickly. I'm not even sure how that giant pig would go about things — I just know it would be painful, ugly, and slow.

Later that day I gave this opinion to a Razorback fan, and he informed me that not only would the giant hog kill and eat me, it would also eat my bones, leaving nothing but my hair, which it would later cough up.

I now consider pigs infinitely scarier than tigers.

The pregame activities included close to 400 Arkansas cheerleaders entering the stadium on top of a giant circus wagon holding the aforementioned killer hog. The wagon stopped, and a man with a microphone told us, "It's time to call the hogs!"

This is perhaps the strangest cheer in the history of humanity, but also the most fun to do. You start with your hands low and slowly raise them to the heavens while saying, "Wooooooooooo." Once at the top, you drop your hands and yell, "Pigs," then pump your right fist and shout, "Sooie!" You repeat this two more times, and on the last round shout, "Razorbacks!" I can't imagine this cheer actually firing up a team, but I guess if I thought actual razorbacks were coming, I'd certainly run faster.

As the game began, it finally dawned on me that I was five hundred miles away from home, watching two middle-of-the-pack SEC teams play before noon. I hate to even say this, but the game was kind of boring. Building on the conclusion I made in Tuscaloosa—that I use Auburn football primarily as a catalyst to increase self-worth—I realized nothing could happen in the Arkansas–South Carolina game that would make me feel better about myself. It was just another SEC game, one of 145 played by SEC teams that year, so I went exploring.

I stood on the concourse for a bit, watching people. Plastic hats shaped like hogs are big in Fayetteville, and I made a note to buy one before I went home. The swine flu pandemic was also a big part of Arkansas fashion. I saw several versions of a T-shirt that said something to the effect of, "I don't have swine flu, I have Hog Fever."

Despite my good seats, I decided to watch the second half from the upper deck. I sat in some overflow bleachers atop the south end zone that feel as if a stiff breeze could blow them clean off the stadium. The Razorbacks kicked off, and South Carolina scored on the first play of the second half, an eighty-yard pass from Stephen Garcia to Alshon Jeffery. But the Gamecocks missed the extra point, and as required by law, everyone in the stadium turned to a neighbor and said, "That might cost them."

It cost them a point I guess, but in the long run it didn't make much difference. The Razorback's gargantuan quarterback Ryan Mallet was a remarkable 23 of 27 for 329 yards, and the home team ripped off twenty-three unanswered points to defeat the Gamecocks 33–16. Sooie.

After the game I walked through campus toward the home of Matthew Chenoweth, a graduate student I'd been talking to since summer. The Arkansas campus is beautiful and has one of the coolest things I've ever seen at any school. The name of every person to ever graduate from the University of Arkansas is engraved somewhere in the sidewalk that winds through campus.

Matthew's house was farther away than I'd realized, but I made it eventually, collapsing into an easy chair just as Alabama and LSU were kicking off.

"I sort of started that whole camping out before games thing," Matt told me. "It was for the Texas game in 2004, and we'd heard rumors people might start camping out for the best seats. So I bought a tent and set up on Wednesday night. Some friends joined, and word got out, and by Friday night there were hundreds of us out there."

"Awesome."

"Not really," Matt said. "By Friday night people were breaking every law in the Bible. We'd unknowingly created a tent city version of Sodom."

"At least you didn't get smote," I said.

"No, but I think God used Texas to punish us the next day."

Matt's roommate Andrew Wise, a Campus Crusade intern and future seminarian, came in from the game, and the three of us watched Alabama and LSU slug it out. The game was tight, and LSU led 15–10 going into the fourth quarter.

It is going to happen, I kept telling myself. LSU was going to pull off the upset, and all my needless worrying about Bama winning the national title would have been just that. But the Tide took a 21–15 lead with ten minutes to play, and when a controversial call negated an LSU interception, I found myself screaming at the television while Matt and Andrew laughed at me. But soon I found myself laughing too, because, honestly, what else could I do? Alabama was good. Very good. And they probably were going to win the national championship. I couldn't do anything about it, and it, I was pretty sure, wasn't going to do anything to me. And by the time I finished the two-mile hike back to my car, I was already over it. Of course that walk included a ten-minute phone call with Tricia that was spent primarily bashing the SEC referees. But hey, like Nick Saban says, it's a process.

Driving back to my hotel, I saw the lights of Bentonville High School in the distance, and at the suggestion of some BYX brothers, I drove by to take a look. If I showed you a picture of this stadium, you would never guess it belonged to a high school. It has a video scoreboard, a massive press box, and what looks like a 100-yard indoor practice facility beyond the north end zone. Auburn doesn't even have a 100-yard indoor facility. And I suppose this would be a good place to rail against the importance our culture puts on athletics, even at the high school level, but I'm too jealous to be indignant.

● ● ●

The next morning I went to the early, early service at Good Shepherd Lutheran Church in Fayetteville. This proved a disservice to the Lutherans, because I didn't fully wake up until near the end of Pastor Dick Jebsen's sermon. But in my defense I had a long drive ahead of me, and the sooner I could be on the road the better. Seriously, that's all I recall, the pastor's name and the name of the church. I think I saw some kids in robes, but that could have just as easily been a dream. It's a shame too, because I know very little about Lutherans, but I promise if I ever return to Fayette-ville, I will attend Good Shepherd at a decent hour and be more attentive.

Driving home, I felt a strange kindredness for the University of Arkansas. Fayetteville reminded me a lot of Auburn, and the people were so friendly and welcoming. I'd like to think I'll go back in future years, but if I'm honest, I'll admit I probably won't. That drive is no fun, and I certainly don't want to travel that far just to see Auburn get its teeth kicked in. So if anyone with power is listening, I think we should let Arkansas go to the Big 12. Yes, we love them. But Drew Barrymore loved E. T., and in the end she knew she had to let him go. Arkansas needs to be in a league with its natural rivals like Texas and Oklahoma, and the SEC needs to add a team that won't embarrass Auburn on an annual basis. I vote for Bentonville High. Actually, let's make that the Bentonville High *JV* team, just to be on the safe side.

Leaving Fayetteville, I stopped at Wal-Mart to pick up a plas-tic hog head as a keepsake. But they were $23.95, and that was a rollback price, so instead I picked up a hog snout for $1.95, then I drove east for fourteen hours. Over the last nine weeks, I'd traveled over 5,500 miles, and it seemed at last I was getting somewhere.

UNIVERSITY OF GEORGIA

NOVEMBER 14, 2009

God is a Bulldog.

Lewis Grizzard

"I DON'T UNDERSTAND why they just didn't run away."

"Because they were in Guyana, in the jungle. If they ran away, they'd just get eaten by jungle beasts."

"But they were going to die anyway, why not run?"

"Because staying is sort of the *point* of being in a suicide cult."

Tricia and I were sitting in Commerce, Georgia's, fabulous Days Inn, watching a History Channel special on Jonestown. You may be too young to remember Jonestown. I am too, so I only know about it because of an awful joke my uncle used to tell.[1] Jonestown, more or less, was an American cult led by Jim Jones, who migrated to South America in the late 1970s to avoid media scrutiny. A congressional delegation was sent to investigate reports of abuse,

---

1. Sorry, Zondervan wouldn't let me tell it here.

and when the delegation tried to leave with two defecting families, cult members shot and killed the congressman and several others. Knowing the end was near for his cult, Jones ordered his followers to drink fruit punch laced with cyanide. Over 900 people committed suicide that day, while Jones shot himself in the head.

It had been a long day, obviously, since the two of us were sitting on a hotel bed watching video footage of a mass suicide. To most people this entire scene would be pretty disturbing, but if I told an SEC fan it all happened hours after Auburn's heartbreaking loss to Georgia, most would say, "Oh yeah, I've been there before."

● ● ●

My day started in an Atlanta hotel with a mind-splitting headache, but after an orange juice and a headache powder (a bad combination, by the way), we hopped on the interstate and drove toward Athens. We last made this trip in 2001, and my memory is of country roads winding into a quaint college town. This morning it seemed like we'd only just left Atlanta when we began seeing signs for the University of Georgia. This is because Atlanta is the kudzu of southern cities. One day soon everything south of Louisville and east of Dallas will be known as Atlanta. Traffic will suck, but what a talent pool for our Little League all-star team!

We got to campus early and drove around looking for a place to park. There were plenty of parking lots downtown, but the only problem was the people standing guard with signs that read, "Parking $40." Seriously, who knew Athens was the lower Manhattan of northeast Georgia? Driving through neighborhoods and back roads, we went under a bridge with a sign that read, "This bridge will eat your bike." I have no idea what that means but hated not to mention it here.

Eventually we decided to leave the car parked on a deserted road about a mile north of campus. We wrote down street names, checked the map on my phone, then started walking toward town, fully aware we'd never see the car again.

Athens is probably best known for its bar scene. In fact, upon enrollment each student is given the deed to a bar downtown. This puts the current number of bars in Athens at 34,885. We were walking among these bars when I got a call from a friend who said he no longer needed the two extra tickets I'd acquired. This wasn't really a problem because I'd only paid face value, and I knew getting rid of them would not take much effort. In fact, the instant I took them out of my pocket and held them aloft, a swarm of scalpers descended upon us, chanting their unceasing mantra of "How many you got? How many you need?"

"I've got two," I said. "And I just want face value for them."

One of the scalpers snatched the tickets from my hand and made me walk about a hundred yards down the street with him. "How much?" he asked.

"I just told everyone I wanted face value."

He looked at the tickets, flipping them over and over in his hands, then said, "You know these aren't really good seats."

"Fine," I said. "Give them back to me then."

"No, face value is cool." Then he waved at another man across the street who walked over and handed me $80 without saying a word. Scalping is so weird.

● ● ●

We had some Georgia fans to meet up with that day, so I called one of them, a guy named Hace Cargo. I don't think that is his real name, probably just something he made up for the book. Hace said he was having lunch with some UGA alumni he knew from Campus Crusade and suggested we catch up at his tailgate after lunch. This was good, because it gave Tricia and me a chance to walk down to Weaver D's.

Weaver D's is a soul food restaurant located just off the Georgia campus. The building appears to be made of cinder blocks and looks a lot like houses I used to build with Legos, except for the fact it is neon green. Outside a sign reads, "Weaver D's Delicious Fine Foods: Automatic for the People." If that last part sounds familiar, it's because the band R.E.M. borrowed the phrase to name their 1994 Grammy-winning album.

The line at Weaver D's wound out of the building, but we didn't have anywhere to be, and once you smell the food it's not like you can just walk away. Slowly we worked our way up to the cash register, where Dexter Weaver, patron saint of Weaver D's, was taking orders. The couple in front of us placed their order, moved to the side, and I found myself face to face with Dexter, who barked out the word, "Communication!" This, I suppose, is how people talk on Dexter's home planet. I stood dumbfounded for what seemed like thirty seconds before finally choking out the words, "Fried pork chop."

Tricia ordered fried chicken, and we joined the line of people waiting for their food. I have to say, even if we'd had to wait a month, the food was worth it. Rarely does a pork chop melt in your mouth, but that was the case with these. And Tricia was thrilled to see a bottle of squirt butter on each table alongside the other condiments. I'm going to go out on a limb and say Weaver D's is not endorsed by the American Heart Association.

I called Hace to get directions to his tailgate, which turned out to be approximately three hours away by foot. This was good, though, because it gave us a chance to burn off at least 1 percent of the calories we'd just consumed. And even though Hace's directions only involved one turn, Tricia and I still managed to get lost, so I sent him a message asking for help.

"Just stop any UGA fan and ask them to point you toward the Varsity."

I replied, "We don't trust UGA fans."

And we don't. On our aforementioned 2001 visit, we'd asked a group of Georgia students for directions following the game, only to be sent to a part of town cops are afraid to drive through.

So, unassisted, we finally found our way to Hace's tailgate, which was actually in the front lawn of the Sigma Phi Epsilon fraternity, where Hace was a brother during his undergraduate years. He is now an intern at UGA Crossroads, which is the name for Campus Crusade at the University of Georgia. During his spare time, he and his friend Stephen Sowell write a UGA football blog called Battle Hymn Notes.

Hace's wife, Sally, walked up and offered us some water, then the four of us talked about football. Hace grew up in a family of Ole Miss and Alabama fans, and naturally he began cheering for those teams as a child, circa 1995. SEC historians out there have probably already deduced that Hace is not a big fan of Tommy Tuberville, the man who left Ole Miss for Auburn in 1998, then later beat Alabama in six consecutive Iron Bowls.

"Tubs was my first hate in SEC football," Hace said.

He went on to tell the story of his freshman year at UGA. "Auburn came to town, and Georgia, with a win, would clinch the SEC's Eastern Division. Before the game some friends and I were circling the stadium, and low and behold there is Tommy Tuberville, conducting a radio interview only a few yards away from where we stood. The rest of my group walked on, but I leaned over the hedges and began to yell his name as loud as I could. *Tommy! Tubs! Tuberville!* This went on for a few minutes. When the interview ended, I started yelling even louder. Then, in an almost magical moment, he looked right at me, probably to see who in the world wouldn't stop screaming his name. In that moment time stood still, and all the hatred, all the terrible things I'd thought about him, and all the times I'd bashed him in conversation—it all came bubbling to the surface. I froze. Then, after a pause that felt like hours, all I could muster was, 'I can't stand you!'"

Tricia and I couldn't stop laughing, in part because we knew Auburn won the game, but also because we could both see ourselves yelling the same thing at Jackie Sherrill if given the chance. "What did Tubs do?" I finally asked.

"He just gave me a confused look, shook his head, and walked away."

Before we left I asked Hace about the spiritual side of things, and he seemed to be dealing with the same things most of us deal with. "At times in the fall it dominates not only my weekends and my Sabbath, but every free moment I have. I'm either reading about football, blogging about it, talking about it with friends, or just sitting around thinking about it. I know that time could be spent on eternal things."

One of the questions I asked myself at the beginning of this adventure was why I wasted time on football when it could be spent on eternal things. It's a question I don't even fully understand. The legalist in me probably thinks it means all hobbies and extracurricular activities should be suspended, and that time should be spent passing out religious tracts at the mall. Of course, that isn't practical, so instead I compare myself to others, and as long as I'm a little more balanced than they are, I feel like I can keep the status quo. But that is childish and perhaps evidence that my relationship with God isn't anywhere near what it should be. Because like I said, the relationship is the key. If it is strong, and if it is what's most important, I think the other things will fall into place. Think of your other relationships, perhaps the one with your spouse. You wouldn't neglect your spouse for days on end because you were on the Internet reading about recruits. Okay, maybe I have done that, but at least you shouldn't do it, and believe me, they will tell you so. I'm not saying God is going to threaten to make you sleep on the couch, though maybe he should. I'm just saying it's no way to treat the most important relationship in your life.

Leaving Hace's tailgate, we walked back down Broad Street, stopping to duck under the Arch, the famous cast-iron gateway to campus. Legend has it that if you walk through the Arch before you receive your diploma, then you will never graduate from the University of Georgia. Another, more peculiar, legend says if you walk under the Arch as a freshman, then you will become sterile. I'm not sure what happens when two Auburn grads walk through, but I suppose our barren children will never graduate from Georgia, which is fine with us. Out-of-state tuition is a bear.

Through the Arch we made our way across the Georgia campus, a campus that seems familiar and foreign all at once. Eight years ago this walk would have led us through a sea of tents whose inhabitants would have barked at us until we were out of sight. Today no one seemed interested. Folks seemed content to eat, drink, and pet their English bulldogs, which run around Athens like squirrels. This indifference toward Auburn fans probably had less to do with goodwill and more to do with Georgia's 5–4 record, but hey, we've all been there. When you're losing football games, you're too busy hating yourself to muster up much hate for anyone else.

With all the walking, our feet started to hurt, and we were tired of not getting taunted, so we stopped by the Tate Student Center, Georgia's impressive student union that had, among other things, a movie theatre showing the Florida–South Carolina game. After watching a few minutes of the game, I tried to call Cody O'Brien, a UGA law student I'd been in touch with.

When we found Cody he was, of course, wearing a hat that read, "Herschel for Heisman." He asked if we'd ever been to Athens before, and we told him once, in 2001. You could see him doing the history in his head, then he shuddered and took a step back. "That game was one of the few times I ever heard my dad curse."

That game was the 2001 Auburn–Georgia game, where then first-year coach Mark Richt inexplicably ran the ball from the three-yard line with ten seconds to play, effectively running out the clock on his own team. I would have cursed, too.

I wanted to meet Cody because on a survey I'd conducted earlier in the summer, he answered the question, "Can prayer change the results of football games?" with, "Who knows? But it sure makes you feel like you are doing your part."

Back we are to our need to feel connected, to feel we are doing our part. I asked a lot of people this fall if they prayed about football. Many said they prayed for a game with no injuries, which is nice, but I could see a child asking, "Why do the big men run as fast as they can and crash into each other and expect not to get hurt?" A few people said they prayed for their teams to play to the best of their ability, which I think is just a sneaky way of praying for a win. And then there was a small minority who actually admitted to asking God to give their team a win. I'm sadly in that small minority, though the prayer usually never gets past me uttering the word *please* over and over again. I figure God knows what I'm talking about. That being said, and I say this with no theological training, praying for your team to win is probably no more effective than wearing your lucky shirt.

Cody kept us in stitches with his stories. He admitted he has thought before that perhaps God would favor the Bulldogs because of Mark Richt's faith, but after seeing the rise of Urban Meyer, Tim Tebow, and the Florida Gators, he no longer believes that way. "I think it's time for Richt to go."

Tricia and I were both shocked to hear a UGA fan say those words.

"Oh, I'm probably the only one here today who thinks that, but we need something new. I mean Richt is a nice guy, but I want my Sunday school teacher to be a nice guy. I want my coach to be a killer."

Cody told us his intensity toward all things Georgia occasionally gets out of hand. "The wife of one of my law school classmates is a huge Bama fan, and the last time I was at their house, I sort of screamed at her. Actually every time I've been to their house I've screamed at her, but she's pregnant this fall, so I've toned it down. A bit."

● ● ●

With the help of Sir Edmund Hillary, we made our way to our seats in an upper-upper deck called the 600 level, a section that was added during our eight-year absence from Sanford Stadium. The good news about our seats was that almost the entire section was Auburn fans. The bad news was that from this height we could actually see the curvature of the earth.

Like everywhere else, the school's band—in this case the Redcoat Marching Band—takes the field for pregame and whips the stadium into a frenzy. But at Georgia all this is paused for a brief moment when 92,746 people extend their arms toward a corner of the upper deck, where a lone trumpeter slowly plays the first notes of the "Battle Hymn of the Bulldog Nation." Then the voice of retired Georgia play-by-play man Larry Munson comes booming through the speakers and says, "Glory, glory to Ole Georgia."

I hate getting goose bumps over other schools' traditions.

Of course, I must admit I kind of like the University of Georgia. Athens is a great town, and had I not gone to Auburn, I could actually see myself as a UGA student. I was baptized by the Rev. Quinn Evans, a Bulldog fan like no other. And the Auburn–Georgia game is perhaps my favorite every year, because while the rivalry is intense, it also feels like family. The great Auburn coach Pat Dye was a Georgia graduate. Georgia's legendary coach Vince

Dooley was an Auburn man. We are like brothers, and I can't tell you how much I was looking forward to seeing Auburn kick its brother's teeth in Saturday night in Athens.

Right on cue, the Auburn offense began the game looking nearly unstoppable. It was 14–0 before you could blink, and high above the earth section 600 was rocking. The Tigers would take a 14–7 lead into the half, and though we had no depth and we knew hanging on in the second half would be tough, Auburn fans remained cautiously optimistic.

My sister-in-law, Lori Dorminey, was head majorette at Auburn in 2000, and she probably won't speak to me next Christmas unless I mention the art of baton twirling. Georgia had a couple of featured twirlers who at one point during the halftime show were twirling four flaming batons. I covered my eyes and peeked through my fingers, knowing they were one bobble away from having to stop, drop, and roll. But these girls were awesome, and their flaming batons never touched the ground or, more important, their hair, much to the delight of the sellout crowd.

The third quarter saw Georgia storm back to take a 17–14 lead, with Auburn kicking a late field goal to tie. During the quarter break, Tricia and I watched UGA (pronounced "ugguh"), Georgia's beloved English bulldog mascot, waddle on the sidelines. If Arkansas' bone-eating pig is the scariest live mascot in the league, then UGA is the mascot whose belly you'd most like to scratch.[2] Georgia scored in the first minute of the fourth quarter, giving me

---

2. UGA VII was only four years old, a puppy, and it's hard to believe just a few days after this game he would die of a heart attack. The next Saturday he would be wrapped in a Georgia flag and laid to rest near his predecessors in the southwest corner of Sanford Stadium. Auburn has a large veterinarian school, and we love our dogs, even UGA, though his ancestor tried to bite an Auburn player in the midnineties. And anyone who has owned a dog knows how hard it is to lose one. On November 19, 2009, the Bulldog Nation lost its bulldog, and throughout the South hearts were heavy.

the sinking feeling the game could get out of hand, just like the infamous Blackout Game from 2007.[3] But Auburn defensive back Demond Washington took the ensuing kickoff and ran ninety-nine yards, tying the game at 24–24.

Momentum went back and forth during the final fifteen minutes, with Georgia finally taking a 31–24 lead on a Caleb King touchdown run. But Auburn wasn't done, and with just under seven minutes to play they began a drive that would put them deep inside Georgia territory. On second-and-eleven from the Georgia twenty-three-yard line, Chris Todd lofted a pass to Mario Fannin near the Bulldog goal line. Fannin had the ball for a millisecond, but Georgia safety Bacarri Rambo delivered a bone-jarring hit that knocked the ball harmlessly to the turf, where Rambo now lay unconscious.

It's amazing how quiet one hundred thousand people can get when a player suffers an injury of this nature. Fans on both sides pray along with their teams, everyone hoping this young man will be okay. And he was okay, suffering only a concussion, though for safety reasons he was taken off the field on a cart, to the thunderous applause of everyone in attendance.

Auburn actually looked more shaken than Bacarri after the play, going backward on third down, taking a false-start penalty, then throwing an incomplete pass to the end zone on fourth down, all but ending the game.

Tricia and I left Sanford Stadium in an angry trot. We were downtown in no time, where jubilant Georgia students were all lining up outside each other's bars. Soon we were searching the back roads for our long-lost car. It took us a while, but we finally found it, and thirty minutes later when we were sitting in traffic, I finally spoke: "I'm not going to the Iron Bowl."

---

3. I've forgiven Georgia for beating Auburn that day, but I will never forgive them for exposing the world to Verne Lundquist's dance moves.

Tricia didn't have a choice. She would be at work the Friday when Auburn would meet Alabama. But I'd planned on being there. I thought it would be good for the book, but now I couldn't imagine watching another Auburn game this season, particularly against an Alabama team that was going to murder us.

"Well, you don't have to," she said.

"I know," I said. "I'm not even sure I want to watch it. But if I do, it'll be in our house, by myself, with the phone unplugged and the blinds closed tight."

We drove in silence out of town and to our hotel in Commerce, where we would watch Jim Jones tell his followers, "Death is a million times preferable to ten more days of this life." It made me feel a little better about things.

● ● ●

Much to my surprise, the sun rose on Sunday morning. Tricia and I got dressed and drove back to Athens to worship with the fine folks of Athens First United Methodist Church. Located in a beautiful building in downtown Athens, First UMC was packed that morning with worshipers wearing red ties, red shirts, and red dresses. Church fashion in the fall is usually a direct reflection of Saturday's scores. I'd packed an orange and blue tie just in case Auburn won, but had opted for a neutral yellow in light of the loss. Tricia, however, had donned a red and black dress for the occasion. I was appalled.

"What are you doing?" I asked.

"When in Rome," she said.

"This is *Athens*."

"It's all Italy."

"Athens is in *Greece*!"

"No one cares, geography boy."

Chuck Hodges, senior pastor of First UMC, took the pulpit

this morning and joked about the amount of antacid consumed by Georgia fans the night before. Then he added, "You know, I have lots of friends who attended Auburn University. They are great people, and Auburn is a great university. And I can't tell you how happy I am to not have to hear how great it is for another year." The crowd howled with laughter, and I discretely slipped my tithe back into my wallet. Okay, that was a lie. I was never really going to give them money in the first place.

• • •

Driving home, Tricia and I rehashed the weekend. We decided it was fun, even though Auburn had lost, and we promised to not wait eight years before returning. As soon as we walked into our house, I deleted the game from our TiVo, a cleansing ritual many of us know all too well. By suppertime I was finally over the game. "You know," I said to Tricia, "I think I'll probably go to the Iron Bowl after all."

"I knew you would," she said.

"How?"

"Because that's sort of the point of being in a cult."

UNIVERSITY OF MISSISSIPPI

NOVEMBER 21, 2009

> To understand the world, you must first understand a place
> like Mississippi.
>
> *William Faulkner*

UNLESS YOU ARE A BRIDE on her wedding day, it's never a good thing to enter a church and have every head in every pew turn and look in your direction. This situation is made particularly awkward when you are white, and everyone else in the church is black. Owing to some bad directions, I showed up to the Spirit of Excellence Church of the Living God at 11:07 for the 11:00 service. Every head turned and . . . well, I'm getting a little ahead of myself here.

● ● ●

This was going to be the game of the year in the SEC. LSU was preseason Top 10, Ole Miss was Top 5. The winner would take the SEC West crown and earn the right to play Florida in the SEC championship game, which these days is more or less a national semifinal. But a funny thing happened on the way to the "game of the century"—if by "funny" you mean five combined losses.

I'd arrived in Oxford at the home of my college roommate, Russell Clayton, late Friday afternoon. Russell is one of those strange people who seems to enjoy school. He already has a master's and is working on a PhD in management at Ole Miss. I, on the other hand, earned a bachelor's degree in philosophy by the edge of Occam's razor. Just the thought of graduate school causes me to hyperventilate.

I was starving by the time I got to Russell's place, so he drove me to Chick-fil-A, which is a fast-food restaurant where Christians eat chicken cooked by other Christians. Since moving to Oxford, Russell has called me at least once a week to lament the fact that his new home did not have a Milo's or a Chick-fil-A, but in the last month a sanctified chicken restaurant was built near his house, and Russell had been tearing it up. "Alicia and I had breakfast here this morning," he told me. "I came here for lunch with some guys from class, and Alicia and I just ate dinner here about an hour before you arrived. This is the fourth time I've been here in twelve hours." Somewhere Truett Cathy is smiling.

On our schedule for the night was a ping-pong tournament for international students at the Ole Miss Baptist Student Union. Russell and I walked inside, and I was shocked at the number of people. At least 60 of the 200 kids looked to be international, making the rest, I suppose, national.

Many of the international students played ping-pong like, well, like you'd expect international students to play ping-pong. One guy would stand up close to the table, slamming the ball with all his might at his opponent, who was standing way back from the table, lobbing every shot back high in the air, where his opponent would slam the ball back again. Russell and I thought briefly about signing up for the doubles tournament set for later that night but reconsidered after a particularly violent slam nearly knocked a kid's eye out.

Matt Metcalf, an Ole Miss senior, was running the tournament. Matt is very involved with the BSU's International Student Ministry, and ping-pong, he told us, was a great way to bring international students to the BSU and make them feel welcome. And he was right, this was probably the most diverse crowd I'd ever seen at a college ministry, and Matt hopes this tournament will continue even after he's gone.[1] Driving home, Russell and I decided we were still a little hungry, so we stopped by Chick-fil-A, Russell's fifth trip of the day, and got milkshakes. Mmm, consecrated milkshakes.

The next morning I woke early and drove to the Huddle House for breakfast with a man named Wilson Defore. Wilson is an Ole Miss alum and a retired surgeon living in Oxford. He spends most of his time these days volunteering with the Ole Miss FCA, mentoring student athletes and learning a thing or two from them. "They are such great kids," Wilson told me. "And being around them has really changed my perspective on things."

"How so?" I asked.

"When you get to know the students, you get to know their needs and what they are struggling with. You see them as people, not just athletes whose sole purpose in life is to entertain you. I pray for them, but not to win games. I don't pray for them to win because I know the players on the other sideline are people too. People with lives and struggles of their own. Who am I to petition God, asking him to let one win over another, just for my entertainment?"

What do you say to something like that? I mean, I know it is true, but it's so much easier to vilify the other team and their fans.

---

1. Not after he's dead, but after he leaves for Nashville to become an accountant.

Maybe if I were to force myself to look at them as people, some of whom are my brothers and sisters in Christ, well, I might be in a much healthier place. And it just so happens that this year some of my brothers in Christ from Tuscaloosa are very good at football. I don't have to like it, but I should certainly get over it, because there isn't anything I can do about it anyway.

Russell and his wife, Alicia, met friends that morning for breakfast—I'll give you one guess as to where they ate—and when they got back, Russell and I hurried over to campus because there was something preposterous I wanted to see.

For years the Ole Miss Band, aka the Pride of the South, had played a song called "From Dixie with Love." From what I understand, the song was a medley comprised of "Dixie," "The Battle Hymn of the Republic," and "Dancing Queen." The problem was some of the more vocal students—and by vocal, I mean drunk—thought the end of this song was a good time to scream, "The South will rise again."

Ole Miss Chancellor Dan Jones decided to put an end to this, first by having the band director shorten the song. It didn't help, and the inebriated minority continued to scream. The Ole Miss Student Government did its part, voting to officially add the phrase "To hell with LSU" to the end of the song, reasoning that wishing eternal damnation on an entire university was slightly better than wishing for the return of the Confederacy. But the new phrase did not stick, and Chancellor Jones made true on his promise to ban "From Dixie with Love" from all Ole Miss sporting events.

However, this did not sit well with Mississippi's number-one consumer of white sheets. The Ku Klux Klan announced just before the Ole Miss–LSU game that they would rally in support of a few loud drunk guys' right to embarrass the university. The statement was from, and I'm not making this up, the Exalted

Cyclops of the Mississippi White Knights (he probably gave up after cutting only one eyehole in his sheet, and the name stuck). Another statement was made by the Grand Titan (he probably studies Greek mythology when not burning crosses), who said the protest would be peaceful. The Honorable Mermaid could not be reached for comment.

The rally was scheduled for 10:00 a.m., and according to the Glorious Unicorn (who has *three* holes in his sheet, obviously), there would be close to 100 Klansmen clad in 400–thread count sheets.

"We aren't coming there to cause problems or cause trouble," said the Grand Titan. "Trouble has already been caused by a handful at Ole Miss, including the black student body president, who wants to shape Ole Miss into yet another liberal sodomite college."

I couldn't help but think the Grand Titan had been misinformed. I've seen plenty of student government elections, and rarely has a candidate run a successful campaign on the promise of more sodomy. I asked my friend Nick Wade, former SGA treasurer at Auburn, if he remembers anyone running on the sodomite platform. "No," he said. "That would never get past the T-shirt committee."

So I found Ole Miss student president Artair Rogers on Facebook and learned his interests are God, spending time with family and friends, and basketball. His favorite book is the Bible, and a quick glance at his campaign website revealed promises of a recycling initiative, a bicycle program, and a young-alumni fair. You know, if I didn't know any better, I'd think the Grand Titan had something against black people.

Russell and I parked a few minutes after 10:00 a.m. and ran across campus to Fulton Chapel, where the Klan rally was to take place. We arrived just in time to see, well, nothing. Just a few people milling around and some police barricades stacked up against a wall. Where was the Exalted Cyclops?

We noticed a few people wearing stickers that read, "UNITY," and I asked one of them what had happened. "Oh there were about ten guys up there in sheets," he said, pointing toward the steps of the chapel. "Half of them looked like kids."

"Did they do anything?" I asked.

"Nope, they stood up there for about five minutes while people stared at them. Some students passed out these stickers, and about a hundred people stood with their backs turned to the Klan, reading the Ole Miss Creed over and over. They all had on T-shirts that said, 'Turn your back on hate.'"

Russell and I found out later that the T-shirts and the back turning were organized by a group called One Mississippi, a campus organization that strives for social integration. Well done, Ole Miss. Well done.

● ● ●

Kickoff was still a few hours away, so Russell and I decided to venture into the Grove. For the uninitiated, the Grove is a shady ten-acre plot in the center of the Ole Miss campus, but on game days it is so much more. On Saturdays in the fall as many as 25,000 fans wedge themselves, their tents, and some of their finest china into the Grove for a tailgating party like no other. Just imagine a refugee camp where UN aid workers were passing out candelabras.

Now I'm not much for crowds, particularly crowds squished together in a confined space, so after about three minutes in the Grove, I was ready to leave. Unfortunately, we were already in too deep. I looked in every direction and all I saw were tents and trees and rebel flags, so I ran. But every turn looked the same, and eventually my world became a terrifying blur of bow ties, argyle vests, and seersucker suits. I screamed for help but was only offered delicious food, which I accepted before resuming my screaming. This was it. I was going to die. "I'm ready Lord; take me!" I screamed.

Nothing happened, so I screamed again, "Lord, I'm ready. Are you ready?!" Then from every direction I heard:

Hellll yes! Damnnnn right!
Hotty Toddy, Gosh almighty,
Who the hell are we, Hey!
Flim Flam, Bim Bam,
Ole Miss by damn!

If this was the Rapture, it had more casual swearing than I'd expected. But it turned out Jesus had not returned — I'd just unknowingly initiated "Hotty Toddy," the famous Ole Miss cheer. This shook me loose from my panic, and I was able to find Russell, who was sitting at the tailgate of his friend Laura Williams.

Laura, or Lulu as I was told to call her, is in the PhD program with Russell. She told us her father and brother were not going to make the game, and the two seats behind her would be open. All we had to do was buy two single tickets, then make our way over to the empty seats. "We sit in an interesting section," Lulu said. "I think you'll enjoy it." This turned out to be the understatement of the fall.

Russell and I went back into the depths of the Grove searching for tickets, and within a few minutes we'd both found one for face value, and since there was still time before kickoff, we decided to stop by the tailgate of Buck and Melanie Ladner. Mrs. Melanie was one of the first people to contact me back in the summer, and throughout the fall she would send me email forwards, each one assuming I was knee-deep in all things Ole Miss.

I am sure you have kept up with Dexter McCluster, who set a school rushing record last week against Tennessee. He was baptized a couple weeks ago at North Oxford Baptist. I'm attaching his testimony.

I am almost certain you have read The Blind Side, *and are looking forward to the film. My brother is a friend of the author, Michael Lewis, and I had to keep it a secret the book was coming out. I am attaching Shepard Smith's interview with Michael Lewis. Shepard is a fantastic Rebel, and is on campus frequently.*

You probably heard about our freshman tailback, Rodney Scott, who lay still at the bottom of a pile while an Auburn player lay on top with a serious neck injury. The doctors say it saved his life. I'll attach the video.

I sent Mrs. Melanie an email the week before the game just to make sure she'd be in town and in the Grove.

"You bet we'll be in town for the game," came her reply. "It's a busy week around here as I'm sure you know. On Thursday our men's basketball team plays Indiana in Puerto Rico at 4:00 on ESPN II. At 6:30 on Friday Coach Nutt will speak to the Quarterback Club, then at 7:00 p.m. he crosses the street to do his radio show. After that we will be attending the opening of *The Blind Side*. We'll be in the Grove early the next morning." I think it's safe to say Ole Miss athletics play a significant part in day-to-day operations at the Ladner home.

At the tailgate Mrs. Melanie greeted us with big hugs and soon was introducing us to everyone in sight. "You're not the only writer here," she said, and walked off to get this mystery author while my mind wandered. Was Michael Lewis here? Was I about to get to meet the author of *Moneyball*, *Liar's Poker*, and *The Blind Side*? Would he give an endorsement for my book? Would we become best friends and vacation together in the south of France? "Chad, I'd like to introduce you to Neal McCready."

Oh, Neal McCready, great.

Okay, I kid. I was excited to talk to Neal. He's a very well-known sportswriter in these parts, but spending summers in Cannes with Michael Lewis was going to be so cool.

Russell told me later that while I was talking to Neal, Mrs. Melanie had asked, "So what is Chad's angle with this?" She wasn't the first person to fear that I planned to write an entire book mocking either Christians or football fans. I guess I just look suspicious.

Russell made Mrs. Melanie feel a little more comfortable talking to me about football, and she told me, "Years ago Buck made veiled threats of divorce because I didn't want to drive to New Orleans for an Ole Miss–Tulane Game. He was joking, but I went anyway." I asked her if the outcome of games upset her, and she laughed. "Look around—this is a social event for me. We live in Oxford, and Ole Miss athletics are a big part of living here. But football is only a game, and I am not my team."

Mrs. Melanie had told me something so simple, yet something I'd failed to grasp. And it doesn't just apply to Oxford or even college towns. If you live in the South, college football is probably going to be a big part of your life, or at least a big part of the life of someone you love. I mean, if you live in Australia, then kangaroos are going to be a big part of your life; and if you live in Iceland, then ice is going to be a big part of your life.[2] And just because something is a big part of your life doesn't make it a sin. Eight days a year Mrs. Melanie eats and fellowships with her friends under a tent in the Grove. Good for her. If I want to do the same in Auburn, it's okay. Sure, if something comes up and I need to miss the game, I should miss the game. But going to the games has never been the problem has it? It's been my constant search for fulfillment away from Jesus Christ. The quicker I learn he is all I need, the quicker I'll be able to enjoy the rest of my life. Which is probably good, because just before I left for Oxford, Tricia got a job offer from a pediatric practice in Auburn.

● ● ●

---

2. Okay, so I'm not very well traveled.

Kickoff was near, so Russell and I made our way to Vaught-Hemingway Stadium. I had a regular ticket and was able to enter the stadium quickly. While I waited for Russell to get through the student line, I was able to figure out just how students were getting their alcohol into the game. I won't reveal their secret here, but I will say it's genius—and that I'm still open to revealing the secret if any SEC school is willing to buy a truckload of my books.

We found our seats just as Dexter McCluster took a handoff fifty-seven yards deep into LSU territory. All around us people were dancing and telling LSU to go to hell.

This was new to me, but Ole Miss and LSU really want each other to go to hell. You see it on T-shirts, buttons, stickers, flags, church signs, and you most certainly hear it in the stands.

Ole Miss had to settle for a field goal, and Lulu began pointing out the regulars in her section. "We call this guy Polka Dot," she said, pointing to the man dancing in the aisle below us. "And that's Shepard Smith's brother next to him. Shepard comes by sometimes—maybe he's here today."

Ole Miss picked off an LSU pass and had two touchdowns called back due to penalties and was now lining up for a forty-five-yard field goal, looking for a 6–0 lead. But the kick was blocked and scooped, and fifty-two yards later LSU was up 7–3. The purple and gold–clad maniacs in the north end zone were bowing in unison, oblivious to those who were chanting for them to take a trip to the infernal regions.

What followed were a few field goals and some touchdowns by both teams, but I wasn't paying much attention, because Shepard Smith, Mr. Fox News, had joined us in the bleachers. And because I'm slightly mesmerized by celebrities, the game was now of no interest to me. I watched Shepard dance with his brother and Polka Dot. I watched him taunt a couple of LSU girls and then pose with them for photographs. I watched him eat some nachos.

LSU took a 17–15 lead to the half, and Shepard left to get food or something. I was depressed, thinking he might not come back for the second half, but he did, and I watched him through most of the third quarter, which saw neither team do anything. But early in the fourth quarter Ole Miss was driving, and when McCluster pulled up on a toss sweep and threw an unexpected touchdown pass, the Rebels had a 22–17 lead. All around people were dancing and singing to "Kernkraft 400," a song you don't think you know, but if you went to a college football game in 2009, you most certainly do.[3] Polka Dot started dancing down the aisle, and we did not see him again for fifteen minutes.

LSU went three and out, and Ole Miss proceeded to use the next nine minutes of game time to drive the length of the field and kick another field goal to take a 25–17 lead with 3:42 to play. The game was over. Shepard Smith began doing an interview with a cameraman who seemed to materialize out of nowhere. "Bye-bye, LSU," he said for his sign-off.

But LSU made a couple of plays, and with less than ninety seconds to go, Jordan Jefferson hit Rueben Randle on a twenty-five-yard touchdown pass. The crowd was in shock. Shepard Smith looked like he was about to throw up. LSU could tie with a two-point conversion, but they missed it, and the crowd erupted again. The game was as good as over, because like I told you earlier in the book, no one ever recovers onside kicks.

Only LSU did, and now all they needed was a field goal to win. Jefferson completed a twenty-six-yard pass, and LSU was in range. Children were crying, men and women were vomiting, and I couldn't take my eyes off Shep Smith. But Ole Miss sacked Jefferson on second down, then blew up a screen pass for a nine-yard loss on third down. It was fourth and forever at the Ole Miss

---

3. Whoa oh oh oh oh, oh. Whoa oh oh oh oh oh oh oh. Whoa oh, ah oh.

forty-eight, and LSU head coach Les Miles let sixteen seconds tick off the clock before calling timeout to set up the Hail Mary.

What happened next instantly became part of SEC lore. Jefferson dropped back and heaved a pass toward the end zone, where Terrance Toliver hauled it in at the six-yard line. Everyone looked at the clock, and there was still a second left. People were screaming while coaches and players were running in every direction. Half of LSU's kick team took the field, then ran off. Jefferson kept looking back at the coaches, the coaches kept looking at the clock, and I kept looking at Shepard, who was screaming at Polka Dot. The referee blew his whistle, the second on the clock ticked off, and Jefferson turned to his coaches with a shrug of his shoulders. The game was over.

Bedlam.

I jumped down from my seat and joined Polka Dot and the Smith brothers for a rousing chorus of "Kernkraft 400," then asked Shep to smile for a photo. He obliged, then grabbed me by the shoulders and said, "Hotty Toddy."

Hotty Toddy indeed.

● ● ●

Later that night Russell, Alicia, and I celebrated the craziest afternoon of my fall with — what else — some blessed chicken strips from Chick-fil-A. Then we took a stroll through the square in downtown Oxford, where Rebels young and old would party late into the night. We stopped in Square Books for some coffee and sat outside on a bench next to a statue of William Faulkner. I told him I had trouble understanding *The Sound and the Fury*. He told me to get the CliffsNotes.

● ● ●

The next morning we ate at Big Bad Breakfast, and afterward the GPS on my phone sent me in the opposite direction of the Spirit of Excellence Church of the Living God. I knew I would be late, and I wouldn't get a chance to talk to anyone before the service to explain why I was there. Sitting in the parking lot, I thought about just leaving and making up an end to this chapter, but I do have *some* artistic integrity, so I walked inside, and every head turned.

But just as quickly their heads turned back to the front, where a band was leading a spirited worship service. I slid into the back pew and clapped along with stereotypical white-boy rhythm. A kind woman walked over to me and said, "You don't have to stand way back in the back." This was true, but I told her I preferred the anonymity of my back pew.

The song ended and another began, followed by another, and then another. I took a quick glance at my watch, and it was already past noon. My preconceptions about African American churches whispered that this service would probably not end before dinner, so I snuck out during prayer.

I'm really not sure what I wanted to happen that morning. Knowing me, I probably thought I could spend an hour in a black church, then write some moving chapter that would heal racial divides throughout the southeast. Yeah, it looks pretty silly when I see it in print. Truth is, I wouldn't even know where to start healing racial divides, though I like to think it could start in the church. Of course 11:00 a.m. on Sunday mornings is perhaps the most segregated hour of the week, so we still have a long way to go.

A pastor asked me this fall if I thought white people in the South thought cheering for black athletes on Saturday excused them from being racist the rest of the week. I told him I'm sure some do, but at least we have four hours of harmony. Forty years ago we didn't even have that. I grew up in a much better Alabama than my parents did, and hopefully my children will grow up in a better one than I did. We still have a long way to go, but maybe we can take a lesson from the Ole Miss students who turned their backs on hate. Hearing of their stand against the Klan warmed my heart.

And it *almost* made me feel guilty for ringing a cowbell seven days later in Starkville. Almost.

MISSISSIPPI STATE UNIVERSITY

NOVEMBER 28, 2009

> Therefore, Rebels, never send to know for whom the cowbell tolls; it tolls for thee.
>
> *John Donne (paraphrased)*

I'D BEEN ON THE ROAD to Starkville for almost an hour when the sun decided to make its daily appearance, and soon its rays were bouncing off the highway and into my eyes. I reached for my Aviators, instantly feeling 43 percent cooler. I was thankful for the level of anonymity the sunglasses gave me as I passed through Tuscaloosa, not that anyone would be awake to give me grief. The roads were deserted, and it felt as if the entire town had only just fallen asleep after a long night of revelry.

My phone began beeping like crazy. I had eight new text messages. Who would be texting me this early? I picked up the phone and opened the messages.

> *War Eagle!!!*
> *Onside kick!!!!*
> *War Eagle Baby!*
> *Noooo!*
> *Sorry Chad!*
> *Sorry dude.*
> *War Eagle anyway!*

This happens sometimes on game days. Messages get stuck in some fourth dimension, only to pop up in your phone days later. Today it felt like getting love letters from a girl who'd dumped me the day before.

● ● ●

Back in the summer, Mississippi State fans were far and away the most enthusiastic about helping with my book. I received dozens of emails from students, alumni, pastors, and fans, all volunteering or volunteering a friend to be part of the MSU chapter.

I was told to spend time with Jason Green, college minister at Meadowview Baptist Church in Starkville, because he coordinates a tailgate tent at home games where people pass out tracts and share the gospel with anyone who will listen. I'd seen something similar to this every week. Men in suits standing on a corner reminding all who passed by of their need to repent, while their wives and children stood nearby holding signs with the go-to phrase, "The End is Near." But Jason's friend Bobby Cole told me this group was a little different. "They have a big tent and offer food to anyone who wants it, and Jason is a season-ticket holder. He loves the Lord and his Bulldogs."

Interesting. Usually these street preachers didn't look like they enjoyed college football—or anything, really, except maybe making people feel guilty. They just saw a crowd of people and decided to go scream at them. So I called Jason, and he confirmed what Bobby had told me. "Yeah, we like to set up our tents and when the college kids pass through on the way to the game we offer them food. It gives us a good chance to tell them about our church and our ministry, then we all go inside and scream for the Bulldogs." As a former college student, I can speak to the subtle genius of this method. If someone had offered me free food, I would have listened to anything — unless the free food was supposed to be washed down with cyanide-laced fruit punch, of course.

Another email came from Dr. Grant Arinder, senior pastor at Calvary Baptist Church in Starkville, and I spoke to him late in the season. "Personally I think I fit the bill," said Grant. "I'm a pastor here, and an avid if not at times rabid fan. But being a pastor I see things daily, from broken marriages to families burying a child, that help me keep things in perspective. I love sports, but for me sports are an escape from my life, they are not my life."

I heard from Will Rambo, a staff member at The Orchard, a Methodist church in Tupelo. Will told me his senior pastor, Bryan Collier, is a Bulldog fanatic and has occasionally been asked to stop jabbing back and forth with the music minister, an Ole Miss Rebel. I spoke to Bryan, and he laughed about it. "Advent starts in the Methodist church on the Sunday after Thanksgiving, which is also the Sunday after the Egg Bowl. One year after a State win, I took the pulpit and began talking about all the things Advent means to me. I said I think of candles, and I think of the advent hymns, and I think of bells, then I pulled my cowbell out from behind the pulpit and started ringing it. But yeah, we've toned it down a bit since then."

Then I got perhaps the craziest email from a man named Owen Cook, telling me stories of Clark Coleman, a Bulldog fan like no other. Mr. Coleman of Yazoo City had just passed away after suffering a massive heart attack. Owen Cook told me, "For the forty-two years I knew him, he was a faithful and ardent Bulldog fan. Whether it was football, baseball, basketball, or any other group that represented MSU, Clark Coleman was 100 percent supportive."

Of all the stories Owen told about Clark Coleman, this was the wildest: "Several years ago Clark was suffering and in great pain. Somehow his intestine had twisted, and he was in serious danger. Riding in an ambulance from Yazoo City to Jackson, Clark refused to allow the medics to give him any pain relievers until they promised not to let any Ole Miss doctors operate on him. Only Dr. Anthony Petro, a loyal Bulldog, was good enough for Clark."

You know, I'd always been told the MSU–Ole Miss rivalry lacked the intensity of other SEC rivalries, but perhaps I'd been told wrong.

●　●　●

A great deal of this preseason excitement revolved around Mississippi State's hiring of Dan Mullen as head coach. Mullen had spent the previous four seasons as offensive coordinator for the Florida Gators, and as quarterback coach he'd mentored such players at Alex Smith, Chris Leak, and Tim Tebow. Unbeknownst to the State fans emailing me in the summer, none of those players were moving to Starkville with Coach Mullen, and by November, the season that started with such hope had been full of disappointments for the Bulldogs. A heartbreaking loss to LSU early in the season was among the lowest points. With first and goal from the LSU two, Mississippi State failed to score on four consecutive plays, causing every fan in the league[1] to simultaneously utter, "Poor State." Later in the season, MSU led #1 Florida 13–10 at the half, only to fade in the fourth quarter and lose by ten. Now

---

1. With the obvious exception of Ole Miss and LSU.

entering the final game of the season, State held a record of 4–7, with no chance of bowl eligibility.

When teams get to that point, they've either quit or become more dangerous than you can imagine.

● ● ●

At 55,082, Davis Wade Stadium is the second-smallest home stadium in the SEC, but its upper decks soar above the Mississippi lowlands, and from a distance you wonder if you're looking at the largest structure ever built.

I followed some cars with MSU flags through campus and parked next to them in a free lot just a short walk from the stadium. Stepping out of my car, I was taken aback by the first cowbell of the day.

Mississippi State fans ring cowbells. A lot. It's sort of their thing. And I'm not talking about two or three of them—all fifty thousand of them ring cowbells. "But aren't artificial noisemakers illegal?" you ask. Why yes, they are, and every two or three years the SEC makes a big deal about enforcing this rule. But the State fans still sneak them in, and security guards still look the other way, and the referees still turn a deaf ear to the thunderous clang.

I followed that thunderous clang up to the stadium, where people were setting up tailgates in the frosty dew. It was freezing, so I started looking for a bookstore or something where I could warm up. Luckily for me, Mississippi State has a massive Barnes & Noble just yards from their stadium. This seemed a little odd, but I was happy to have shelter from the cold. I ordered a cup of so-much-chocolate-and-caramel-you-can't-taste-the-coffee, and then I called Matt Loving, Next Generation Pastor at CrossPoint, a Southern Baptist church in Starkville. Matt had invited me to CrossPoint's tailgate, and he said they'd just set up tents and I'd better hurry over because breakfast was served.

CrossPoint's tailgate was on a hill looking back down toward Davis Wade Stadium. Matt explained I'd just walked through something called the Junction, a large park where thousands of tailgaters were set up this morning. "There used to be six roads that met right there," Matt told me. "It was called Malfunction Junction because no one understood who had the right-of-way and people were constantly having wrecks. The school decided to make this a park and reroute the streets."

I fixed myself some breakfast, and Matt introduced me to some folks from CrossPoint. The first couple I met was Beverly and Mack Lowry. The two of them had already had an interesting morning. "She threw our tickets out with the garbage yesterday," Mack said.

"Wow," I said, wondering how they were managing to laugh about it. "I think technically you have biblical grounds for divorce."

Turns out Mississippi State has some understanding folks in the ticket office, and the Lowry's tickets had been replaced. "What happens," I asked, "if you get to your seats and find two people covered in garbage holding your old tickets?"

Beverly laughed and said, "If they want the seats that bad, then they can have them."

● ● ●

Before heading in to the stadium, I called Morris Morrison, father of our good friend Jenny. I'd met Morris back in the summer at Jenny's wedding, where he was wearing a Mississippi State belt. Jenny told us her parents go to every State home game and tailgate with friends from Harrisburg Baptist Church in Tupelo. I knew he'd be here today for the Egg Bowl.

"I'm sorry, Chad. We're actually in San Antonio this weekend."

Jenny, like Tricia, is a pediatric resident, meaning she gets about four free hours a year to see her family. This year her four free hours were the same weekend as the Egg Bowl, and as much as Morris loves his Bulldogs, he loves Jenny more.

"We've got the TV ready though," he told me. "It's going to be a great day."

I didn't want to keep Morris away from family time, but I wanted to get a feel for this rivalry, so I asked him to quickly tell me about his feelings toward Ole Miss.

"Oh, we hate them," he said, and then he laughed. "But you know, we have lots of dear friends who went to Ole Miss, and we really do love them. But we hate them too."

Now it was getting close to 11:00 a.m., so I decided to head inside Davis Wade Stadium and take my seat. I found it way over in the corner of the south end zone, just a section away from the Ole Miss band. Sitting down, I began flipping through my program, when suddenly a man tapped on my shoulder. I looked up to see a family of four looking at me, then at their tickets, then back at me. "I think you may be in our seats," the father said.

"Maybe so," I said, showing him my ticket.

"Yeah, this is Section B," he said. "You're in Section A," and he pointed toward the Rebel Band.

I apologized and walked over to Section A, only to find my seat was in the row directly behind the Ole Miss tuba section.

The seat wasn't bad really, so long as the band wasn't playing, but that's the thing—bands play constantly. I love marching bands. I think they're one of the things that make college football unique. Marching bands are the condiments on our football burgers. That being said, I hope I never sit this close to one again. I couldn't even see the State players perform the Dawg Pound Rock, a pregame dance so strange that seeing it live probably wouldn't have helped me explain it here. On the field I didn't miss too much though, as an Ole Miss field goal was the only score of the first quarter.

Both teams kicked field goals in the first five minutes of the second quarter, and Ole Miss led 6–3, but then State took the ball and drove eighty-one yards for the game's first touchdown. Davis Wade was rocking and the cowbells were ringing; but just before the half, Ole Miss receiver Shay Hodge made the catch of his life, and the Rebels took a 13–10 lead into the locker room.

The third quarter was all Bulldogs. MSU took the opening kick and drove to the Ole Miss thirty-one before kicking a game-tying field goal. A quick three-and-out by the visitors and State began a seven-and-a-half-minute, thirteen-play drive to take a 20–13 lead. Those folks that had doubts entering the day were starting to believe. Their faith was boosted when Charles Mitchell picked off a Jevan Snead pass on the next possession, returning it to the Ole Miss thirty-four-yard line. And just before the quarter ended, Chris Reif hit Chad Bumphis on a fourth-and-nine pass. Bumphis fought off what looked like every Ole Miss defender, then raced into the end zone. It was 27–13 Bulldogs. The tubas finally sat down.

But this was a rivalry game, and if anyone thought Ole Miss was done, they were sorely mistaken. In fact, forty-five seconds after the Bumphis play, Jevan Snead hit Markeith Summers on a forty-eight-yard touchdown pass to cut the lead to seven. Around the stadium blood pressures were rising. This is where State would collapse—you could almost feel it coming. But no one told the Bulldogs, who seven plays later were dancing in the end zone with a 34–20 lead.

Panic set in on the Ole Miss sideline. They were down two scores with only ten minutes to play. The next drive began, and for a minute the Rebels looked poised to march down the field, but things stalled, and on fourth and seventeen MSU defender Corey Broomfield jumped a Jevan Sneed pass. Broomfield then raced sixty-four yards for the Bulldog touchdown.

I have so many memories from my season on the road in the SEC, but probably none of them left quite the impression on me as the State crowd's reaction to Broomfield's interception return that put the Bulldogs up 41–20.

Davis Wade Stadium erupted, spewing Ole Miss fans out to their cars. The clanging was so loud that not even Christopher Walken could have asked for more cowbell. I'll never forget the Mississippi State drum major, trying to direct the band while jumping around on her podium, holding her head in disbelief. The joy was so contagious that for close to an hour I completely forgot Auburn had lost the Iron Bowl the day before. It was like when the Apollo astronauts circled around to the dark side of the moon and lost radio contact with mission control. For a few glorious moments, I was so happy for someone else I forgot to be sad for myself.

Ole Miss would score again in the next thirty seconds, but it didn't matter. The game was over. State drove down to the Rebel goal line and took a knee, sparing their rival the humiliation of another score. A photo of MSU running back Anthony Dixon flashed on the JumboTron, and below him were the words, "From Dixon with Love."

The few Rebel fans still in their seats began to leave. Some of them got in shouting matches with Bulldog fans. I don't mention this to speak poorly of Rebel fans, because fans of every school do this. It's hard to make that long walk from a stadium and endure the taunts coming from all around. But Rebel fans asking State fans what bowl game they'd be playing in wasn't going to stop those in maroon from pointing at the scoreboard, which read "Mississippi State 41 That School Up North 27."

I kept my seat in the Ole Miss section, which was now empty. State fans kept looking in my direction, hoping to taunt me, but my yellow shirt and seeming indifference probably led them to believe I was, at least, not an Ole Miss fan. A man came out with the Golden Egg, the trophy these two teams have played for since 1927. He handed the trophy to Coach Dan Mullen, who handed it off to his players, who paraded it around the stadium to the delight of everyone. I waited until the last player exited the field and walked out of an SEC stadium for the last time in 2009. The Junction now looked like a Mardi Gras parade.

I walked back up the hill to CrossPoint's tailgate, which was now even larger than before. Matt pointed out the senior pastor, Scott Cappleman. "He's a Rebel fan. Maybe you should get his opinion on the game."

Scott was not weeping and tearing his garments, so I figured he was safe to talk to. "It was an exciting game," he told me. Huh?

"I have split loyalties. I pull for both Ole Miss and Miss State, but when they play I have to pull for Ole Miss, which doesn't always go over very well when you are a pastor in the heart of Bulldog Nation." I looked around, but no one was getting in Scott's face or giving him grief about the game.

He must have noticed my puzzled look. "Oh, they're always great to me. I just have to remind them we are a community of grace, so sinners and Rebels are both welcomed at CrossPoint."

Sometime around five that evening I left campus. Grills were lit, food was cooking, and the party showed no signs of ending anytime soon. Mississippi State had beaten Ole Miss, and all was right in the world.

Driving back to my hotel, I called my friend Matt Haines, pastor at Sixth Street Baptist Church in Alexander City, Alabama, and 1990 graduate of MSU.

"What a game," he said.

"It was a lot of fun," I told him. "Did you think you guys had a shot?"

"After two years ago, I know better than to lose faith."

"The punt-return game?"

"Yeah, I was there with my two sons, Nathan and Andrew. My brother Brad had already left our seats because he was so angry. We had played awful, and it was 14–7 with about six minutes to go. I told my boys we were going to leave, so we walked down from our seats and stood in the end zone, watching the game on the JumboTron, ready to bolt for the car when I knew the game was lost. Nathan, my oldest, kept saying, 'But, Dad, the game isn't over yet. We can still win.' So we force Ole Miss to punt with a little over two minutes left, and sure enough Derek Pegues takes that thing up the middle and goes seventy-five yards for the score. I'm going nuts; I grab my boys, and we run back to our seats—the whole time Nathan is screaming, 'I told you, Dad, I told you we could win!' We got the ball back, drove down and kicked the game-winning field goal with ten seconds left. All the way home Nathan kept saying, 'I knew we could win. I told you, Dad. I knew it.'"

I suppose if you are going to be a State fan, it's best to have the faith of a child.

● ● ●

That night I sat in my hotel room watching *SportsCenter* and eating Krystal burgers. I was tired and a little lonely, but had Tricia been there we certainly would not have been eating Krystals, so I suffered the isolation for my reward of small, squared deliciousness. Watching the highlights from rivalry weekend, I thought about all the new friends I'd met.

Vanderbilt was 2–9 and I hoped Joe Thomas had not hurt himself. Over in South Carolina, Mr. Haynes had just seen his fifty-sixth USC–Clemson game, and his Gamecocks had won big. I wondered if my Tennessee friends were finally warming up to Lane Kiffin, and the answer was no. In Baton Rouge folks were still talking about last week's debacle, and it looked like Les Miles would spend the next season on the hot seat. Tim Tebow was taking the field for the last time in the Swamp, and his Gators would unleash Old Testament wrath on Florida State. Up in Lexington the Big Blue Nation was getting ready for a bowl game, but more important, basketball season. In Arkansas the Hog fans were still trying to get the paint off their chests. The Georgia Bulldogs were wrapping up a lackluster season by defeating their two biggest rivals—not bad for an off year. And back home Tide fans were getting ready to play Florida in a rematch of last year's SEC championship game, while Auburn fans were licking their wounds.

Alabama had defeated Auburn 26–21 the day before in a game that broke my heart. My Tigers jumped up 14–0 early and led the game for fifty-eight minutes, but the Tide scored in the final minutes to secure the win. Bama players left the field to the thunderous applause of the Crimson faithful; Auburn players limped off to the rousing chants of, "It's great to be an Auburn Tiger"; and I drove home with the radio off, trying to swallow the disappointment. But when I got home, I did something I don't think I've ever done before: I watched the replay on TiVo. The kids had played so hard, and the atmosphere had been so incredible, I just wanted to see it again. The next morning the loss still stung, but not like it used to. Looking back, I'm even thankful I was there, because it sure was something to see. Nothing beats rivalry week.

● ● ●

The next morning I went to spoken Eucharist at the Episcopal Church of the Resurrection. The service was quiet and reflective, though I could still hear cowbells ringing in my ears. Communion was offered, and my Episcopal friend from work told me it was okay for a Baptist to partake, so I partook, and bleeehhh—real wine. How about a little warning for those of us used to grape juice?

During a breakfast fellowship, I spoke to Rev. Lee Winter, the parish rector. "I served as Rector of Emmanuel Episcopal Church in Opelika during the mid-eighties," he told me. "The football over in Alabama is crazy. Here things are not as intense; it's not quite as important." Then, without missing a beat, he pointed to the snack table and asked, "Could I offer you a piece of maroon and white cake or some Bulldog biscuits?"

After a slice of maroon and white cake, I got in my car and drove home one last time. It had been, without a doubt, the most interesting football season of my life, and now it was over. Almost.

POSTSEASON

SWEET HOME ALABAMA

One's destination is never a place, but a
new way of seeing things.

Henry Miller

IN ALABAMA THERE'S AN OLD JOKE folks love to tell about a man and
his preacher discussing football.

"Aren't you just appalled," asks the man, "at the amount of
money these people are giving to the athletic departments at Alabama and Auburn?"

"Appalled?" asks the preacher. "On the contrary, I'm encouraged by it."

Confused, the man asks, "Why would you be encouraged by it?"

"Because," the preacher says. "People should give to their religion."

We laugh because there is some truth in what the preacher
says, but football isn't *really* our religion, is it? You'd be hard-
pressed to find someone out there who'd actually admit as much.
"No," we say. "Christianity is our religion, and Jesus is our Savior."

And we mean it, but do our actions match our words?

The week before the Iron Bowl, Tricia and I were having dinner with some friends when they shared some troubling news. "Our Sunday school class volunteered to work in a soup kitchen the morning of the Alabama game."

"What?" Tricia said, not hiding her disgust.

"Seriously?" I asked. "Are they trying to run people off?"

"We wouldn't go," we told them. "They should know better."

You don't know how embarrassing it was to type that conversation. They should know better than what—feeding the homeless? I can tell you all day football isn't that important to me, but my actions are speaking so loud you'd never hear my words.

● ● ●

A few days after the season, I recalled this conversation, and it sickened me how callous my response had been. I felt like I'd come so far through the season, and still I caught myself slipping back. But surely I hadn't driven more than 6,000 miles just so I could recognize when I'm being a jerk. Self-awareness is great and all, but I was hoping for some substantial, permanent change. I guess I still had some things to talk through, so I called my pastors.[1] First, I talked to Dr. Terry Ellis, former pastor of Spring Hill Baptist in Mobile, where Tricia and I were members during her medical school years. He didn't answer but returned my call the following evening, jokingly chastising me for calling during a Kentucky basketball game.

I asked what he learned about faith and football from ten years of preaching in Alabama. "It's very real to people," he told me. "Very important. You know we used to laugh about planning church events around football, but we don't even laugh about it anymore, we just do it. If your event goes up against Auburn or Alabama, your event is going to fail." Then he made an interesting point. "You have to go back a few decades, but communities used

---

1. Yes, I have more than one.

to gather around the church. Now we gather around our sports teams. We live in a sports culture."

If that is true—if we live in a society that revolves around sports—then it's no wonder I keep turning to football for things only God can provide.

Next I called Dr. Gary Fenton, senior pastor at Dawson Memorial Baptist Church in Homewood, Alabama. Dr. Fenton has lived in Alabama for over twenty years now, after growing up in the Midwest. I heard he was a big Oklahoma Sooners fan, and I hoped maybe he could shed some light on my troubles, though I was apprehensive about talking to a man who could compare my tithing record to the price of season tickets.

We met in Dr. Fenton's office and I told him about the book and my recent travels, wondering if he would scream at me for missing thirteen consecutive weeks of church at Dawson. He thankfully refrained and instead asked what I'd learned about myself over the course of the season. I told him how I look to football for my joy in life, and how so much of my self-worth is wrapped up in the wins and losses. He laughed.

"Just this year," he said, "I had to sit down and tell myself that football is only a game, and my happiness does not depend on its outcome. Sure, I love the Sooners, but they are not the source of my joy." Then he smiled and said, "I count it pure coincidence this great revelation came to me while our Heisman-winning quarterback was being helped off the field with a season-ending injury."

There was some comfort in knowing the pastor of one of Alabama's largest churches knows my struggles. In the back of my mind, I've always thought there might be a switch I could flip that would instantly make me the mature Christian I often long to be. As if one day I would wake up and my struggles would be gone without a trace. But Dr. Fenton said "just this year" he had to remind himself that football is not the source of his joy. And I think what he was really saying to me was, "remind yourself daily." Going forward, I hope that is something I can practice, particularly on game days. Those Saturdays always seem so rushed, but what would happen if I took a little time in the morning to thank God for letting me enjoy the day and the game with people that I love? Not only that, but what if I asked God for perspective to help me remember football is only a game, and that he loves me whether my team wins or loses? I get the feeling it's the kind of prayer God would be happy to answer.

Looking back, I believe Dr. Fenton could have talked me through most of my problems, but instead I spent the rest of our meeting asking him impossible questions about Calvinism.[2]

● ● ●

On December 5, 2009, I was sitting next to my Grandpa James in his room at Gadsden Regional Medical Center. His heart was failing, and earlier in the week he'd given my mother instructions not to bury him on Saturday because #2 Alabama was playing #1 Florida, and he'd hate to think he kept people from watching the game. But he made it to the weekend, and despite his depressing surroundings, I could see in his eyes the excitement of a child. His Crimson Tide was about to win the SEC, there was no doubt.

"Don't you want to stay and watch the game with us?" he asked with what might have been a smirk.

"No." I laughed. "That game is the last thing I want to see."

He laughed too, and then I hugged his neck and told him I loved him.

Grandpa was scheduled for pacemaker surgery the following Monday. I was worried about him, but he *had* been hospitalized at least five times a year for the past five years, so I wasn't that worried. Besides, if Alabama was going to play for the national championship, he was going to live to see it.

Leaving the hospital, I drove by Crestwood Cemetery to visit

---

2. Is Lane Kiffin more totally depraved than most people?

Uncle Jimmy's grave. Standing over his headstone, I read the familiar dates, then scraped the dirt from the tiny football engraved below his name. I thought about saying something, but I'm not sure he's talking to me after my conversion to Auburn. So I just knelt there until I got cold, then drove north to Nashville.

I could offer some lame excuse about why I didn't attend the SEC championship game. Maybe something about fearing the corporate atmosphere of a championship game would provide a disappointing ending to my book. But the truth is I just didn't want to see Alabama beat Florida, so I drove back to Vanderbilt to watch my friends in Original Cast perform their 2009 Fall Show.

I'd planned to have dinner at the Pancake Pantry, even leaving myself enough time for the hour wait, then I'd head over to the show, which was called "Someday Just Began." While driving I listened to a Francis Chan podcast, anything to avoid the game, and after fighting through construction traffic, I finally parked at 6:30, prepared for deliciousness.

I can't recall what I saw first. The Closed sign on Pancake Pantry's window, or people rushing out of the bars up and down Twenty-first Avenue. I stared at the window in disbelief, then turned just in time to hear the first "Roll Tide" echo through the dark Nashville skies. Alabama had won the game 32–13. I ate at McDonald's and tried not to sulk.

I would later learn Florida QB Tim Tebow, he of Scripture-based eye-black, had chosen John 16:33 for this particular game: "In this world you will have trouble." Thanks, Tim. You picked a great time to break out the self-fulfilling prophecies.

The Original Cast show was great, and I enjoyed it immensely, even though Alabama was going to play for the national championship. Show tunes, it seems, can get anything off my mind. My only slip was during intermission, when I heard the houndstooth-clad woman in front of me ask her friend, "Did we win?"

"Yes! 32–13!"

"Roll Tide!"

I wanted to scream. You don't get to be part of the "we." Not if you don't even know if your team won the SEC championship game. Of course, I'm no more a part of my team than she is of hers, but I suppose God will forgive my occasional slipup. I did compose myself and change seats, but not before a blood vessel burst over my eye.

Afterward I spoke briefly to my friends, congratulated them on an amazing show, and then drove back to Birmingham. And driving home I couldn't help but think of all the Bama fans in my life, many friends, old and new, and my family, including the woman who brought me into this world. I knew they were dancing in the streets, and the least I could do was be happy for them. So I tried.

● ● ●

I wonder sometimes what it would be like to live in Nebraska or Louisiana. Those fans have an entire state to themselves. Sure they have rivalries, but for the most part they don't have to see rival fans on a daily basis. Being part of this Alabama-Auburn thing has made life twice as difficult as it should be. Worrying about my own team takes up enough time, but I spend just as much time worrying about Alabama. I know Tide fans will call this LBS (Little Brother Syndrome), but I thought about Auburn just as much growing up an Alabama fan. It seemed that for my happiness to be complete, not only did my team have to be winning, but my rival had to be annihilated.

Consequently the rivalry brings out the worst in me as a person. It brings out the part of me that refused to revisit a church after the pastor said "Roll Tide" from the pulpit. And the part of me that will not sing the words "Look! There is flowing a Crimson Tide" whenever the organ plays "Grace Greater than Our Sin."[3] Just before Christmas my friend J. T. asked if I'd concede Alabama's national championship if it meant this book would be

---

3. However, I will shout, "Sin had left a crimson stain," when we sing "Jesus Paid It All."

a *New York Times* Best Seller. "Of course not," I said. "What's the point of having a bestseller if the world is ending?"

But that was my problem—thinking a football game will change my life, when truthfully it changes nothing.

● ● ●

When Texas QB Colt McCoy was knocked out of the BCS championship game with a shoulder injury, I was once again in a hospital room. This time I was watching Tricia hold Jake Dawson Dorminey, our nephew, who was born on the morning of Alabama's thirteenth national championship. I looked over at Lori and Johnny, the two proud parents, and Colt's injury didn't seem to dampen their joy, so I tried not to let it dampen mine.

In fact, earlier that morning I got a call from my mother. She and Grandpa James had just returned from the cemetery, where they'd placed crimson and white shakers on Uncle Jimmy's grave. It had been a rough month for my grandpa: a pacemaker had helped his heart, but a diagnosis of inoperable lung cancer weighed heavy on us all. Alabama winning this game would mean so much to him. I tried to keep that in mind as the Tide rolled.

We got home just in time to see Marcel Dareus pick off a Texas pass, perform a 300-lb. pirouette, then rumble into the end zone to give Alabama a 24–6 lead. I knew my friend Hunter Johnson, who is slightly obsessed with the Tide defender, had probably passed out from elation. Texas would come back to make a game out of it, but we missed most of it. Tricia had recently accepted the job in Auburn, so we turned off the game and shopped for houses online. Of course, we checked the news before going to bed, and like we thought, Alabama had beaten Texas 38–21. The Crimson Tide were national champions.

I went to bed that night with a strange mixture of relief and embarrassment. The worst thing that could happen for an Auburn fan had just happened, and it appeared life was going to go on. No one had come to burn down my house. I still had my health, my dogs still loved me, and in nine months another football season would begin, hope springing eternal around the league.

In Pasadena and Tuscaloosa and little towns across Alabama, men, women, and children would be dancing late into the night. Across town at Brookwood Hospital, Lori and Johnny were holding their newborn son, happier than all of the Bama fans combined. In Glencoe my uncle Wayne was fighting back tears as he told Grandpa James, "You did it, James. You lived to see another Alabama championship." To which my grandfather replied, "Yes I did, and I think I want to live to see another one." And at our little house in Birmingham, I lay in bed next to my wife, finally realizing, it is only a game.

● ● ●

I talked to Jeff Norris, Campus Crusade director at Alabama, a couple of weeks after the BCS Title Game. "Do you know what I got when Alabama won the national championship?" he asked. "A T-shirt and a special edition of *Sports Illustrated*, and I had to buy those."

"So all the problems in your life didn't magically disappear when Coach Saban lifted the trophy?"

He laughed. "No. But that's okay. The season was great, and I made great memories that will last a lifetime. In John 6:35 Jesus says he is the bread of life, and if you come to him, you will never be hungry. I think what he is saying is the things of this world aren't made to fill us up. If we try, they will only leave us feeling empty. And that's the paradox for us sports fans. Had I been waiting for this national title to give my life meaning, the morning after the game would have been a tremendous letdown. But I'm in a healthy place these days, and because I wasn't looking to the game as the source of my joy, I enjoyed it that much more."

"That's so cool," I said. "I hope when Auburn wins the national title, I'm able to enjoy it like that."

"Well, you guys might want to hurry up," Jeff said with a laugh. "Jesus isn't going to wait forever."

● ● ●

Sometime after the Alabama–Tennessee game, I hit my low point and began hiding Bama fans on Facebook and Twitter. One person I hid was Mac Powell, lead singer of Third Day, whose Alabama tweets were more than I could handle. But a few days after the BCS game, I unhid everyone and realized Mac and David Nasser had actually been to Pasadena for the big game. If you are not familiar, David Nasser is an Iranian-born speaker, author, and minister, and judging from his tweets, he appeared to be an insufferable Bama fan. I called him that afternoon.

David agreed to meet with me at his office in Hoover, Alabama. Literally within seconds he was ragging me about Auburn's lesser-tier bowl game. I thought about leaving. But then David spoke seriously: "As an evangelist I'm always looking for a way in to people's lives, a conversation starter. With football in the South, two men can be complete strangers one minute, and if the topic of football comes up, they'll be talking like old friends."

I told David about some of the problems I've faced with sports, and how at times it has bordered on idol worship.

David nodded and said, "This is what I tell people. If you have this much passion for football," and he stretched his hands out wide, "I say great. Stay that passionate about football." Then he stretched his hands as far as they would go and said, "Be this passionate about God."

David went on to echo Jeff Norris's thoughts on what the national title had done for him. "I try to make a few games each year, but the fall is my busiest season, and it's not always easy.

This year I was able to see the final four games. Mac and I even had sideline passes for the SEC championship, and once we won that game, there was no doubt we had to go to Pasadena. So we went, and we screamed till we lost our voices, and I came home the exact same person I was when we left." Then he added with a laugh, "Only my wallet was significantly lighter."

I thanked David for his time, and as I was leaving he said, "You know who I pray for? I'm praying for those fans who woke up the morning after the bowl game and realized despite the win, they still lack peace. Football is a great hobby, but a horrible god."

● ● ●

Football is a horrible god. This one sentence sums up everything I learned in three months of traveling. I know, not really a mind-boggling revelation, but replace football with other words like my spouse, my job, or my church, and soon you discover the problem we all face. Nothing on earth was made to take the place of God in our lives, but we seem hell-bent on trying them all.

You know, I struggle with the concept of grace. Many of us do. To me, the idea of Karma makes much more sense. I want formulas. I want a Bible verse that says, "If thou goeth to a game of football, then thou shalt pray seven times, and thou shalt giveth an hour's wages to the needy among you." But that's not the way things work, and I struggle with it.

Sometimes I feel guilty, because in my mind I have constructed a god who fills the earth with wonderful things, only to become angry when we enjoy them. I should be thankful for football. Thankful I live in the American South, where I can enjoy the passion and pageantry of a game like no other. And thankful this game, fantastic as it is, is not my god.

Maybe after all this I'm finally getting there. It's the only way to explain what happens next.

EPILOGUE

GRANDPA JAMES DID NOT ATTEND the University of Alabama, and he was never wealthy enough to give barrels of cash to the athletic department. He never held season tickets, and it's doubtful anyone on campus, apart from his granddaughter, even knows his name. He is just a fan, like so many others, who enjoyed watching football games with his son.

For his entire adult life, Grandpa worked in Gadsden's Goodyear tire plant, providing for his children opportunities that he never had. A generation later his first grandchild would graduate from Auburn University, a shock, no doubt, but he was there in Beard-Eaves-Memorial Coliseum when I received my diploma, and he could not have been prouder. "I've been trying to cheer for Auburn," he told me once. "I know how much it means to you, but I'm having a hard time." I nearly cried. "Pa, you don't have to cheer for Auburn. I understand." He looked like a two-ton weight had been lifted off him.

My life has been richly blessed, thanks in part to the foundation Grandpa James laid for our family. I've met coaches, players, and athletic directors. I've watched games from the sidelines and from luxury boxes. I've been to closed practices and once even knew an onside kick was coming twenty-four hours in advance. Just this year I saw all twelve SEC stadiums, something my grandfather still cannot believe. He introduced me to the game I will follow all my life, and it was time I did something for him.

On Tuesday, February 2, Mom and I drove my grandfather to Tuscaloosa for the first time in sixteen years. He thought I needed to go for my book and that he was just tagging along. Tommy Ford, my friend in the athletic department, met us at the side door to the Mal M. Moore Athletic Facility. We took an elevator up to the second floor, and when I wheeled my grandfather out, he was face-to-face with the BCS National Championship Trophy.

"We wanted you to see this, Pa," I told him.

He slowly stood from his wheelchair and walked closer to the beautiful crystal football. Then he turned around misty-eyed, smiled, and said, "This sure is something to see."

Mom took some pictures of Grandpa and the trophy, then asked me to stand next to him, but I refused. "I'll wait until Auburn wins one," I said. They all laughed and patted me on the head.

Next we wheeled him down through the weight room, and up another elevator to see Mark Ingram's Heisman Trophy. Again he stood up for a closer look, this time nearly setting off an alarm on the trophy.

Tommy then showed us the practice fields, the recruiting lounge, and the window to Coach Saban's office. Then we went across the street to the Paul W. Bryant Museum, and I pushed my grandfather around the displays.

"You don't remember this one, do you?" he asked, pointing at an old game program.

"No," I said. "And neither do you—that game was played in 1922." He just laughed.

But as we made our way through the museum, the games became more recent. Grandpa was visibly emotional at times, hanging his head and wiping his eyes. We made it to the 1980s and he asked again, "Do you remember this one?"

I did. I remembered riding in the back of that old station wagon to Legion Field. I remembered catching Van Tiffin's field goals during warm-ups. I remembered Jimmy accidentally throwing me into the ceiling fan when Bama blocked Penn State's field goal in 1989. I remembered George Teague stripping the ball from Lamar Thomas in the Sugar Bowl. And I remembered Jay Barker bringing me to tears three months after Jimmy died.

"Yes, Pa, I remember all of them."

In recent months my grandfather found an old trivia book Jimmy gave him just before he died. He takes it with him to his favorite bench in the Gadsden Mall, and whenever someone sits to rest, he quizzes them with slightly dated Alabama trivia. When we loaded up to leave Tuscaloosa that day, I handed him a copy of Tommy Ford's *Alabama Vault* book. "This is for you," I told him.

Grandpa flipped through the book, shaking his head at the memories inside. He took his washcloth and held it over his eyes for a moment, then finally said, "This was all for me today, wasn't it? You did all of this for me."

"Yes, sir, I did."

He shook his head again, then smiled and said, "I love you so much, son. Roll Tide."

I hugged his neck and said, "I love you too, Pa. War Eagle." Four months later he was gone.

AFTERWORD

On Wednesday, February 3, one day after I took my grandfather to Tuscaloosa for the last time, Auburn signed what many are calling the greatest recruiting class in school history, including the five-star quarterback I jokingly mentioned praying for throughout this book. Excitement over the 2010 Auburn Tigers has already reached fever pitch. I covet your prayers.

For more information on Chad's latest exploits, or to contact him, please visit www.chadgibbs.com.

GLOSSARY

Amsterdam Café: My wife's favorite restaurant in Auburn. She is hoping if I mention them here she will get a lifetime supply of turkey wraps.

Athens: A town in northeast Georgia made up entirely of bars.

Bully: Mississippi State's live bulldog mascot. Lesser known than UGA, but more famous than Tyler, the University of Arkansas at Monticello's live boll weevil.

Calhoun's on the River: A Knoxville restaurant with great food, and the perfect strategic position from which to attack the Volunteer Navy.

City Grocery: A restaurant in Oxford, Mississippi, that reportedly serves the best shrimp and grits on earth. I tried to get reservations on two days' notice, but they laughed at me.

Cockaboose: A series of old railroad cabooses that have been converted into tailgating condos outside Williams-Brice Stadium in Columbia. I would include a picture, but seeing them wouldn't help you make sense of them.

Colonel Reb: Former Ole Miss mascot who was, for reasons of racial sensitivity, banned from the sidelines in 2003. In March 2010, a student movement in Oxford pushed to have Colonel Reb replaced by Admiral Ackbar, the fish-headed leader of the Rebellion in *Return of the Jedi*.

Dreamland: BBQ joint that originated in Tuscaloosa, Alabama. Visit www.dreamlandbbq.com to have some ribs sent right to your door.

"Dynamite": Vanderbilt University's fight song, which contains the unfortunate line, "down the field with blood to yield."

Florida Gators: The football equivalent of that kid in your neighborhood who had all the cool toys, including the giant G.I. Joe aircraft carrier.

Geaux: Louisianan spelling of "go." As in, "Geaux get my wallet, I'm gonna make this guy an offer for his wife."

Golden Egg: Willy Wonka's gift to the winner of the annual Mississippi–Mississippi State game.

Groucho's Deli: Sandwich shop in Columbia, South Carolina. Get the Apollo Dipper and thank me later.

Hace Cargo: Member of the Faith and Fanaticism Tour all-name team. Others include Cass Trumbo, Adair Poschel, Andy Enkeboll, and Diggity.

Houndstooth: Black-and-white check pattern made famous in the South by Alabama coach Paul "Bear" Bryant, then made more famous by those two blonde chicks they show on TV every Saturday.

Muscadine Ripple Ice Cream: Delicious ice cream flavor served at the Cheese Store in Starkville, Mississippi. They also had Sweet Potato–flavored, but I'll let you try it first.

Original Cast: Vanderbilt University's Broadway revue troupe. Learn more at http://studentorgs.vanderbilt.edu/originalcast.

Pancake Pantry: Nashville restaurant that apparently serves tasty pancakes, but I can't say for sure.

"Rocky Top": Sometimes mistaken for the Tennessee Fight Song, "Rocky Top" is a favorite in Neyland Stadium, though it is likely to get you shot in Bryant-Denny Stadium.

Roll Tide: Words my children will identify with the taste of soap.

"Sandstorm" by Darude: Perhaps the most techno of all techno music, and a fan favorite in Williams-Brice Stadium.

Seventh Day Adventists: NFL fans.

Scalpers: People who wonder how many you've got and how many you need.

Skullet: A hairstyle popular with John Biery, and no one else I can think of.

Sooie: Something yelled to encourage the Arkansas Razorbacks, or to call a 500-pound wild boar.

Swine Flu: Favorite illness of T-shirt makers in Fayetteville, Arkansas.

Tent City Version of Sodom: The overnight line for the student section at the University of Arkansas. When fire from the sky one day consumes Fayetteville, blame Matt Chenoweth.

Thanksgiving: A very difficult holiday in Alabama due to its proximity to the Iron Bowl. Once while serving turkey and dressing, my mother-in-law screamed at her brother because he wouldn't stop degrading Auburn quarterback Dameyune Craig.

The Grove: The result of Ole Miss fans thinking the outdoors needed to be fancier.

The Rock: A boulder, roughly the size of a Wal-Mart, on the Tennessee campus in Knoxville. On Fridays in the fall The Rock is decorated for the following day's game. The rest of the year it is used for all sorts of things, from welcoming freshmen, to wishing people happy birthday, to informing the world that your ex is a tramp.

The Swamp: A great stadium that I will unfortunately forever associate with the smell of vomit.

"Tiger Rag": A song used by Pavlov in one of his experiments. Whenever it is played, LSU fans begin to foam at the mouth.

Toomer's Corner: The corner of College Street and Magnolia Avenue in Auburn. It has been designated a family-friendly vandalism zone by the city.

Trifecta: Picking the win, place, and show in correct order on a horse bet. I nearly won $25,000 at Keeneland on a trifecta, but trying to collect on a near trifecta proved difficult.

Tropical Storm Chizik: A storm of biblical proportions that struck Jordan-Hare Stadium on the night of September 19, 2009, destroying $79 in property, namely my grey New Balances.

Tusk II: The University of Arkansas' 400-pound live Russian boar. Tusk II died on January 5, 2010. This I suppose should have been as sad as UGA dying, but if I'm being honest, that pig scared me to death.

UGA: The University of Georgia's live English bulldog mascot. UGA VII passed away during the 2009 season and was replaced temporarily by Russ, which is a funny name for a dog.

Volunteer Navy: An awesome tradition, but perhaps the least formidable navy to ever sail the seas.

Xbox 360: A complicated video gaming system used by college kids to embarrass Tecmo Bowl legends.

ACKNOWLEDGMENTS

Now for my acknowledgments, which will be extensive, but I'm operating under the assumption that if you put someone's name in a book they are more likely to buy it.

War Eagle to my wife, Tricia. You warned me not to put anything mushy here, so I'll resist. Just know that I love you more than Cadillac Williams, which is a lot.

Roll Tide to my grandfather, James Parrish. Even though we cheer for different teams, I never watch a football game without thinking of you. May you rest in peace.

Roll Tide to my mom, Kim Gibbs. Thank you for still loving me, even after I came out of the closet wearing orange and blue.

War Eagle to my dad, Alan Gibbs. I'm glad to have you on my side during the holidays.

Go Knights to my editor, Angela Scheff. I'm so thankful no one had to try and read this book before you made it readable. Please know I only partially blame Auburn's Iron Bowl loss on your attendance.

Hook 'em Horns to Donald Miller, Go Ducks to Jordan Green, Go Beavers to Karen Spears Zacharias, and Never Give Up, Never Surrender to Andy Meisenheimer. This book would not exist without your help and encouragement over the past four years.

Go Ducks to my agent, Chip MacGregor. Thank you for your tireless work, and for answering even my dumbest questions.

Go Vols to Dudley Delffs. Thank you for believing in this book. I hope it fares better than Lane Kiffin.

War Eagle to my Lord and Savior Jesus Christ. I know you are probably not an Auburn fan, but sometimes it's fun to pretend.

And a big thanks to Becky Shingledecker/Philpott, Mike Salisbury, Tom Dean, Jeff Gifford, Don Gates, and all the folks at Zondervan who made this book possible.

● ● ●

You cannot write a book like this without a lot of help from a lot of people. Okay, maybe you can, but I can't, so please indulge me while I thank those people who helped me at each stop on my journey.

Go 'Dores to my Vanderbilt friends:

Fr. John Sims Baker, Rick Britton, Lance Brown, Brennan Carmody, Ginger Carr, Carter Crenshaw, Stacey Croft, Spencer Crosswy, Andy Enkeboll, Mark Forrester, Carrie Fry, Maggie Hawk, Jason Ingalls, Billy Ivey, Ken Locke, Jeff Markle, Aaron Moscow, Jonathan Payne, Steve Spencer, Joe Thomas, Tom Tyndall (Go Gators), Alison Wenzel, Malcolm White, Sean P. Williams, Oliver Wolfe, BXY, Campus Crusade for Christ, Original Cast, Vandy+Catholic, Vandy RUF, Wesley-Canterbury Fellowship, West End Community Church, Sister Commodore

War Eagle to my Auburn friends:

Josh Agerton, Rux Bentley, Lynn Blount, Kyle Bradberry, Bill Boldt, Brant Bonds, John Ferguson, Belon O. Friday, Mark Gibbs, Archie Jordan, Jeffrey Lee, Bryan Matthews, David Olive, Orange Jumpsuit Guys, Chris Rushing, Scott Seitz, Chase Strickland, Steve Thompson, Patrick Tyndall, Jim Weeks, Chris Wilson, David R. Wilson, Rachel Winter, Baptist Campus Ministry, Campus Crusade for Christ, Cornerstone Church, First Presbyterian Church, Lakeview Baptist, and all my e-friends on the Auburn message boards (I'd list you all by username, but that would be weird)

Go Cocks to my South Carolina friends:

John Abercrombie, Daniel Brand, William Buddin, Ce Buddin, Fred Byrd, Jimmy Easterby, BJ Estes, Bonnie and Jack Haynes, Jeremy Laughead, Devin Olenick, Tony Sisk, Tim Stewart, Brock Warner, Eric Wenger, Campus Advance, Columbia Church of Christ, Columbia Midtown SDA Church, First Presbyterian Church of Columbia, Gamecock BCM, Oliver Gospel Mission, Shandon Baptist, Steve Spurrier's visor

Go Vols to my Tennessee friends:

Gary Brown, Joe Carcello, Meggan Clements, Sam Darden, Clark Davidson, Diggity, Heather Godsey, Brent Harriman, Neyland Lipham, Tim Miller, William Pender, Mike Plewniak, Amy Rosenbaum, Chris Sells, William Shiell, Nathan Simmons, Eva and Victor Thompson, Tameka Tift, David Wells, Mike Wenger, John Wood, Alpha Omega, Birmingham Big Orange Club, Cedar Springs Presbyterian, Christian Student Fellowship, Cornerstone Church of Knoxville, Park West Church of God, RUF, The Walk, Volunteers for Christ, Wesley Foundation, Lane Kiffin

Geaux Tigers to my LSU friends:

Max Adams, Maggie Bowles, Fr. Gerald Burns, Kristi Denton, Deacon Richard Grant, Vick Green, Britteny Kelley, Josh LaRavia, Nathan Marceaux, Steve Masters, Taylor Matthews, John Miller, Dan Ohlerking, Stephen Picard, Gregory Pitcher, 220, Baptist Campus Ministry, Campus Crusade for Christ, Healing Place Church, St. Aloysius Catholic Church, St. James Episcopal, The Chapel, The Refuge, Huey P. Long

Go Gators to my Florida friends:

Zach Allen (Go Noles), J. W. Arnold, Kevin Bird, Emily and Pat Brown, Cody Davidson, David Fuquay, Eddie Gilley, Anthony Gratto, Brian Hinote, Beverly and Don Holt, Kaleb Irwin, Michael Kuhn, Ron Kuykendall (Go Mountaineers), Steve Lammers, Jonathan Morton, Jimmy Trent, Dean Tzobankis, Julie Vaiarella, Brett

Williams, David Wood, Baptist Campus Ministry, Campus Church of Christ, Campus Crusade for Christ, FCA, Gator Wesley Foundation, North Central Baptist Church, Pentecostals of Gainesville, RUF, St. Andrews, the kid who puked on me

Roll Tide to my Alabama friends:

Trae Durden, Tommy Ford, James Goodlet (Go Jackets), Joel Gorveatte, Barbra and Michael Green, Dennis Harkey, Hunter Johnson, Billy Jones, Patrick Laney, Christie Lehren (Go Dawgs), Tim Lovett, John Lowe, Gil McKee, Ryan Moore, Scott Moore, Jeff Norris, Keith Pugh, Gary Rutledge, Doug Smith, Kelli Stringer, Brant Waddell, Bama Crusade, Baptist Campus Ministry, Calvary Baptist, First Baptist Church Tuscaloosa, First Presbyterian Church Tuscaloosa, First UMC Tuscaloosa, First Wesleyan, Open Door Baptist Church, RUF, Westminster Fellowship, Mount Cody

Go Cats to my Kentucky friends:

John Biery, Mariska Coetzer, Nate Collier, Tim Cooper, Gavin Duerson, Ben Frasier, Billy Frey, James E. Haubenreich, Kelly Holderman, Jason Hyatt, Brian Marshall, Tony Neely, Dexter Speck, John Strange, Bryan Taylor, Kevin Wooten, Broadway Christian Church, Campus Crusade for Christ, Cats for Christ, Christian Student Fellowship, FCA, Secretariat

Woo Pig Sooie to my Arkansas friends:

Matthew Chenoweth, Jordan Difani, Spencer Hansen, Matthew Harding, Brad Harris, Keith Hoggard, Jim Hyde, Paul Sagan (Go Rebels), Chris Swain, Cheryl Sybrant, Kevin Trainor, Cass Trumbo, Association of Baptist Students, BYX, Campus Crusade for Christ, Central United Methodist Church Fayetteville, Covenant Presbyterian Church, Cross Point Community Church, First Baptist Church Springdale, First Christian Church Fayetteville, Good Shepherd Lutheran Church, John Daly

Go Dawgs to my Georgia friends:

Katie Branscomb, Dann Brown, Hace Cargo, Walker Keadle,

Cody O'Brien, Bart Scarborough, Charles Simpson, Solomon Smothers, Stephen Sowell, Blake Underwood, Athens First United Methodist, Campus Crusade for Christ, Episcopal Center @ UGA, Georgia Christian Student Center, Sigma Phi Epsilon, Early Cuyler

Hotty Toddy to my Ole Miss friends:

Wilson Defore, Laura Gettys, Isaac Jenkins, Buck and Melanie Ladner, D. Merricks, Neal McCready, Matt Metcalf, Taylor Moore, Janet Oller, Artair Rogers, Joshua Smith, Shepard Smith, JT Taylor, Lulu Williams, Baptist Student Union, Campus Crusade for Christ, Spirit of Excellence Church of the Living God, St. Peter's Episcopal, Wesley Foundation, William Faulkner

Go State to my Mississippi State friends:

Grant Arinder, Michael Ball, Joey Beck, Scott Cappleman (Go Rebels), Bobby Coleman, Bryan Collier, Owen Cook, Tim Cummings, Joy Davis, Josh Gilreath, Jason Green, Matt Haines, Matt Loving, Bill Mauldin, Morris Morrison, Steve Phillips, Jamie Phipps, Will Rambo, Nathan Taylor, Baptist Student Union, Calvary Baptist Church, Crosspoint Church, FCA, First Baptist Starkville, Harrisburg Baptist Church, Meadowview Baptist Church, The Orchard UMC, Christopher Walken

● ● ●

And finally thanks to all my friends and family who helped with this book in one way or another. You guys are the best!

Jon Acuff, Jon Adams, Bryan Allain, Sam Allison, Ashleigh, Morgan, Garrett, and Beau Ashley, Clark Bailey, Mary Baird, Amber and Jason Battles, Sarah Grace and Patrick Beverly, Allison and Zac Boman, Jason Boyett, Brian Brown, Haley Burford, Burnside Writers Collective, Melanie and Kevin Burson, Lori and Jeremy Burns, Hillary and Justin Campbell, Stacey and Kevin Carden, Chris Cate, Alicia and Russell Clayton, Sarah and Jason Cook, Kathryn Corey, Anna and Ryan Cothran, Nick Davis, Karen and Harrell

Day, Amanda and Rees Denham, Aaron Donley, Lori, Ava, Jake, and Johnny Dorminey, Eric Ellis, Terry Ellis, Sandy and Matt Estes, Rachel Held Evans, Gary Fenton, Natalie and Adam Fulgham, Missy Garner, Chris Gary, LeAnn Gentry, Sam and George Gibbs, Glaze-Swedenburg Sunday school class, Benji and Amanda Green, Erik Guzman, Gina and Brian Harris, Leslie and Chris Harrison, Catherine Hartman, Jenny and Kelly Heegard, Amanda and Michael Helms, Staci and Daniel Henson, Whitney and J. T. Hornbuckle, April and Jonathan Hollingsworth, Susan Isaacs, Craig Jordan, Linda Kay, Adam Kidd, Keat Litton, Meredith and Hays Latimer, Paul Loyless, Traci and Charles Marsh, Kristen McDonald, JD McDuffie, Jacque and Jonathan Middleton, Brooke and Josh Miller, Mary Leah and The Rodney Miller, Michael Morris, Bo Morrisey, David Nasser, Kate Nielsen and my friends at CFGB, Jordon Orr, Melissa and Adam Pierce, Ashely and Kyle Powell, Lauren and Nick Rachel, Sam Rives, Tara and Scott Robinson, Megan Roggendorff, Jordan Ross, Emily and Hugh Rushing, David Shaul, Ben Shell, Rob Stennett, Erin and Scott Stephenson, Judy and Steve Stocks, Lisa and Michael Strane, Allen Sullivan, Jarrett Tate, Matthew Paul Turner, Shannon and Griff Tyndall, Harper and Bob Vance, Eric Wade, Volree and Nick Wade, Patrick White, Kelly and Adam Williams, Sarah and Billy Wilson, Dawn Wingard, Susan and Nick Wintermantel, Justin Zoradi and the good people at These Numbers Have Faces (www.thesenumbers.org), and to all my family and friends, past and present, who have blessed my life so richly. I love you all.

● ● ●

Undoubtedly I have left someone out, and I'm sorry. But if an apology is not enough, and if you didn't feel adequately thanked by the "family and friends past and present" line, then feel free to fill in your name below.

And last but certainly not least, I want to thank _____. You'll never know how much you mean to me.